Youth Gang Programs and Strategies

U.S. Department of Justice
Office of Justice Programs
Office of Juvenile Justice and Delinquency Prevention

Summary

◆

John J. Wilson, Acting Administrator
Office of Juvenile Justice and Delinquency Prevention

August 2000

U.S. Department of Justice
Office of Justice Programs
Office of Juvenile Justice and Delinquency Prevention
810 Seventh Street NW.
Washington, DC 20531

Janet Reno
Attorney General

Daniel Marcus
Acting Associate Attorney General

Mary Lou Leary
Acting Assistant Attorney General

John J. Wilson
Acting Administrator
Office of Juvenile Justice and Delinquency Prevention

This document was prepared under cooperative agreement number 95–JD–MU–K001 from the Office of Juvenile Justice and Delinquency Prevention (OJJDP), U.S. Department of Justice.

Points of view or opinions expressed in this document are those of the author and do not necessarily represent the official position or policies of OJJDP or the U.S. Department of Justice.

The Office of Juvenile Justice and Delinquency Prevention is a component of the Office of Justice Programs, which also includes the Bureau of Justice Assistance, the Bureau of Justice Statistics, the National Institute of Justice, and the Office for Victims of Crime.

Foreword

The growth of youth gang violence and the proliferation of youth gangs into smaller cities and rural areas in recent years have focused public attention on the youth gang problem and made it an increasingly significant social policy issue. The public's concern is understandable, with more than 800,000 gang members active in over 3,000 gangs according to the latest National Youth Gang Survey. The Office of Juvenile Justice and Delinquency Prevention (OJJDP) shares this concern and is addressing it on several fronts, in particular, through OJJDP's National Youth Gang Center.

Youth Gang Programs and Strategies draws on more than a half-century of gang program evaluations to summarize what we have learned about:

◆ Prevention programs (including early childhood, school-based, and afterschool initiatives).

◆ Intervention programs (including those that work to create violence-free zones, establish gang summits and truces, and rehabilitate gang members in juvenile detention and correctional facilities).

◆ Suppression programs (including those focused on prosecution, police response, and geomapping and other tracking systems).

◆ Strategies using multiple techniques (such as community policing).

◆ Multiagency initiatives (including local, State, and Federal efforts).

◆ Comprehensive approaches to gang problems (such as the Comprehensive Community-Wide Approach to Gang Prevention, Intervention, and Suppression).

◆ Legislation (at the local, State, and Federal levels).

This Summary also describes an OJJDP-sponsored nationwide assessment of youth gang prevention, intervention, and suppression programs; debunks prevalent stereotypes surrounding youth gang members; and provides research-based recommendations for enhancing the effectiveness of youth gang programs and strategies.

Youth gangs imperil not only the safety of America's communities but the future of our Nation's youth. I trust that the information provided in these pages will improve our efforts to combat this danger.

John J. Wilson
Acting Administrator
Office of Juvenile Justice and Delinquency Prevention

Acknowledgments

A number of people have been instrumental in helping to improve this Summary's quality and in bringing it to completion. John J. Wilson, Acting Administrator, Office of Juvenile Justice and Delinquency Prevention (OJJDP), made very helpful suggestions. Betty Chemers, Deputy Administrator of Discretionary Grants, OJJDP, played a key role in reconceptualizing its format to facilitate use by practitioners. James Burch, Program Officer, OJJDP, provided text material describing OJJDP's five-site Comprehensive Community-Wide Approach to Gang Prevention, Intervention, and Suppression and was especially helpful in improving the final version of the Summary. Phelan Wyrick served as the Program Officer for the National Youth Gang Center project, made valuable contributions, and helped expedite its publication. Other OJJDP staff also made helpful comments. Ellen McLaughlin of the Juvenile Justice Clearinghouse masterfully reorganized and edited the manuscript and coordinated the production of the Summary.

Several colleagues helped make significant improvements to this Summary. Bruce Buckley, Lee Colwell, David Curry, Malcolm Klein, Cheryl Maxson, Walter Miller, Joan Moore, John Moore, Jim Short, Jr., and Barbara Tatem Kelley provided very helpful comments on earlier drafts. The author also is grateful to National Youth Gang Center staff for their helpful review comments. In addition, Rolf Loeber and David Farrington reviewed and provided very insightful comments on a portion of the material in this Summary in the course of editing *Serious and Violent Juvenile Offenders: Risk Factors and Successful Interventions* (Loeber and Farrington, 1998). The author's chapter in that publication—which also is in the Final Report of the OJJDP Study Group on Serious and Violent Juvenile Offenders (Loeber and Farrington, 1997)—contains some of the material in this Summary (see Howell, 1998a).

Table of Contents

Tables and Figures

Tables

Figures

Introduction

Youth gang problems have grown significantly in the past 25 years (Miller, in press). During this period, both the number of cities with reported youth gang problems and the number of gang members have increased nearly 7 times, while the estimated number of youth gangs has increased more than 10 times (Miller, 1992; Moore, 1997; Moore and Terrett, 1998; Office of Juvenile Justice and Delinquency Prevention, 1999; National Youth Gang Center, 1997). In the past few years, however, more recent surveys suggest that the percentage of jurisdictions with active youth gangs is decreasing slightly, from 53 percent in 1996 to 51 percent in 1997 to 48 percent in 1998 (Moore and Cook, 1999). The estimated number of gangs and gang members also decreased during this period (by 7 and 8 percent, respectively).

Without a clear understanding of why and how youth gangs form, preventing their formation is an intricate and challenging task. Gangs emerge, grow, dissolve, and disappear for reasons that are poorly understood. This lack of understanding impedes efforts to prevent gang emergence, disrupt existing gangs, and divert youth from them. Youth gang research must continue to address how gangs form, how existing gangs can be disrupted, and how youth can be diverted from joining gangs.

Evaluation of youth gang programs and strategies is an equally complex undertaking. Their effectiveness must be assessed not only in regard to the formation and dissolution of gangs and the diversion of youth from gangs, but also in regard to delinquency and crime prevention or reduction. Because each youth gang and each community is unique, finding similar groups and communities for comparison is difficult. Measurement problems also plague gang research. Because there is no commonly accepted definition of "youth gang," comparison of study results is problematic. Furthermore, because gang interventions are rarely based on theoretical assumptions, measurement of what these programs are attempting to accomplish is difficult. Most important, very few rigorous scientific evaluations have been undertaken.

Definition of "Youth Gang"

The term "youth gang" is commonly used interchangeably with "street gang," referring to neighborhood or street-based youth groups that meet "gang" criteria. However, the lines between youth gangs, street gangs, and organized criminal enterprises are often blurred (see Klein, 1995a). For the purposes of this review, Miller's (1992:21) definition of "youth gang" is applicable: "a self-formed association of peers, united by mutual interests, with identifiable leadership and internal organization, who act collectively or as individuals to achieve specific purposes, including the conduct of illegal activity and control of a particular territory, facility, or enterprise." Motorcycle gangs, prison gangs, racial supremacists, and other hate groups are excluded. Likewise, gangs whose membership is restricted to adults and that do not have the characteristics of youth gangs are excluded (see Curry and Decker, 1998). Unless otherwise noted, the term "gangs" as used in this Summary refers to youth gangs.

This Summary outlines programs and strategies that have been and are being used to break the lure and appeal of gangs and reduce gang crime and violence. Evaluations and national assessments of some of these programs are discussed, and an overview of what practitioners and administrators need to know before designing and implementing any gang program or strategy is provided. Although several gang programs have been evaluated (see table 1), only a few programs are presented here; information on others is available in *Serious and Violent Juvenile Offenders: Risk Factors and Successful Interventions* (Howell, 1998a)

and in the Youth Gang Consortium Survey of Gang Programs.[1]

---

[1] This information is available electronically at the National Youth Gang Center's (NYGC's) Web page, which can be accessed at www.iir.com/nygc/. The consortium consists of Federal, State, and local agency representatives. This survey, which does not necessarily list *proven* programs but ones that some agencies have implemented in response to gang problems, was conducted by NYGC on behalf of the Youth Gang Consortium. In addition to a description of consortium members' gang-related programs and funding levels, contact information is provided. Eight other publications are available that detail the history of youth gang programming, including what has not worked and why (Bursik and Grasmick, 1993; Conly, 1993; Curry and Decker, 1998; Goldstein and Huff, 1993; Howell, 1998a; Klein, 1995a; Spergel, 1995; and Needle and Stapleton, 1983).

Table 1. Selected Gang Program Evaluations, 1936–99

Program	Study	Design	Type of Intervention	Results
New York City Boys Club*	Thrasher, 1936	Descriptive and case study	Prevention—general delinquency	Negligible impact
Chicago Area Project (CAP)	Kobrin, 1959; Schlossman and Sedlak, 1983	Descriptive and case study	Prevention—community organization	Indeterminable
Midcity Project (Boston)	Miller, 1962	Field observation and quasi-experimental	Prevention—community organization, family service, and detached worker	Negligible impact
Chicago Youth Development Project*	Caplan et al., 1967; Gold and Mattick, 1974; Mattick and Caplan, 1962	Quasi-experimental community comparison	Prevention—detached worker and community organization	No differential impact
Chicago YMCA Program for Detached Workers*	Short, 1963; Short and Strodtbeck, 1965	Field observation and quasi-experimental observation	Prevention—detached worker	Early results encouraging; no final results: evaluation suspended
Group Guidance Project (Los Angeles)	Klein, 1969, 1971	Quasi-experimental	Prevention—detached worker	Significant increase in gang delinquency
Ladino Hills Project (Los Angeles)	Klein, 1968	Quasi-experimental	Prevention—detached worker	Significant reduction in gang delinquency
Chicago Community Action Program (Woodlawn Organization)*	Spergel, 1972; Spergel et al., 1969	Descriptive statistical trends	Social intervention	Ineffective
Wincroft Youth Project (U.K.)*	Smith, Farrant, and Marchant, 1972	Quasi-experimental	Prevention—detached worker	No differential impact
Gang Violence Reduction Program (California)	Torres, 1981, 1985	Quasi-experimental	Suppression and crisis intervention	Declines in gang homicides and intergang violence
House of Umoja (Philadelphia)	Woodson, 1981, 1986	Descriptive, case study, statistical trends	Prevention, crisis intervention, and social intervention	Effected truce among warring gangs; effective sanctuary
Operation Hardcore (Los Angeles)	Dahmann, 1981	Quasi-experimental	Suppression (vertical prosecution)	Successful gang prosecution process
San Diego Street Youth Program*	Pennell, 1983	Quasi-experimental community comparison	Prevention—detached worker	Indeterminable
Crisis Intervention Services Project (Chicago)	Spergel, 1986	Quasi-experimental community comparison	Crisis intervention and suppression	Some reduction in serious and violent crimes
Broader Urban Involvement and Leadership Development (Chicago)	Thompson and Jason, 1988	Quasi-experimental school comparison	Prevention—discouraging adolescents from joining gangs	Marginal reduction

continued on next page

Table 1. Selected Gang Program Evaluations, 1936–99 (continued)

Program	Study	Design	Type of Intervention	Results
Youth Gang Drug Prevention Program (Administration on Children, Youth, and Families)*	Cohen et al., 1994	Quasi-experimental treatment and control comparison (multiple sites)	Prevention—discouraging adolescents from joining gangs; community mobilization	Little or no effect on gang involvement; some delinquency reduction
Aggression Replacement Training (Brooklyn)	Goldstein and Glick, 1994; Goldstein, Glick, and Gibbs, 1998	Quasi-experimental treatment and control comparison	Skills training, anger control, and moral education	Preliminary results positive with members of 10 gangs
Tri-Agency Resource Gang Enforcement Team (TARGET) (Orange County, CA)	Kent and Smith, 1995; Kent et al., 2000	Quasi-experimental	Suppression—targeting gang members for prosecution, supervision, and incarceration	Successfully targeted hardcore gang members and showed serious crime reduction
The Neutral Zone (State of Washington)	Thurman et al., 1996	Direct observation, focus group, and crime statistics	Prevention and alternatives to gang involvement	Some positive results (but see Fritsch, Caeti, and Taylor, 1999:26)
Montreal Preventive Treatment Program	Tremblay et al., 1996	Longitudinal study from kindergarten; random assignment	Prevention via skills development (in prosocial skills and self-development)	Reduced delinquency, drug use, and gang involvement
Little Village Gang Violence Reduction Program (Chicago)	Spergel and Grossman, 1997; Spergel, Grossman, and Wa, 1998	Quasi-experimental community comparison	Social intervention and suppression	Positive results; best results with combined approach
Youth Gang Drug Intervention and Prevention Program for Female Adolescents* (Pueblo, CO; Boston, MA; and Seattle, WA)	Curry, Williams, and Koenemann, 1997	Quasi-experimental	Prevention and social intervention	Pueblo program showed positive results with culture-based programs for Mexican American females
Gang Resistance Education and Training Program (G.R.E.A.T.)	Winfree, Esbensen, and Osgood, 1996; Esbensen and Osgood, 1997, 1999	Quasi-experimental treatment and control comparison (multiple sites)	Prevention—discouraging adolescents from joining gangs	Modest reductions in gang affiliation and delinquency
Gang Resistance Education and Training Program (G.R.E.A.T.)	Palumbo and Ferguson, 1995	Quasi-experimental and use of a focus group (multiple sites, different from G.R.E.A.T. sites above)	Prevention—discouraging adolescents from joining gangs	Small effects on attitudes and gang resistance
Operation Cul-De-Sac (Los Angeles)	Lasley, 1998	Quasi-experimental before, during, and after comparisons with control area	Suppression—using traffic barriers to block gang mobility	Gang homicides and assaults appeared to be reduced
Antigang Initiative (Dallas)	Fritsch, Caeti, and Taylor, 1999	Quasi-experimental; compared target and control areas	Suppression—using saturation patrol, curfew, and truancy enforcement	Aggressive curfew and truancy enforcement appeared to be effective

* These programs are not described in the main body of the Summary.
Source: Adapted from Loeber and Farrington, 1998.

Programs and Strategies

In the sections that follow, gang programs and strategies are described in seven major categories: prevention, intervention, suppression, programs using multiple techniques, multiagency initiatives, comprehensive approaches to gang problems, and legislative approaches. When available, evaluation results are presented.

Early in the Nation's history, youth gang work emphasized prevention. These programs were followed by interventions designed to reintegrate particular gangs into conventional society using "detached workers" (agency representatives dispatched from their offices to work directly with gangs in the community). Detached workers were sent out in automobiles to intervene in crisis situations. A major shift then occurred as programs, led by the police, sought to suppress youth gangs, buttressed by enhanced legislative penalties for gang crime. Currently, a mixture of approaches is being tried across the Nation; however, programs that integrate prevention, intervention, and suppression activities are gaining popularity.

This Summary includes multiple techniques that some jurisdictions use to achieve prevention, intervention, and suppression program goals—such as providing alternatives to gang involvement while employing suppression to make gang life unattractive. Other jurisdictions incorporate multiagency suppression initiatives involving several law enforcement agencies, perhaps in multiple jurisdictions. Many jurisdictions are taking a comprehensive approach by integrating prevention, intervention, and suppression strategies. Finally, some jurisdictions attempt to suppress gangs by passing legislation or city ordinances prohibiting gang involvement or directed toward specific crimes.

Prevention Programs

The history of gang intervention in the United States shows that early programs emphasized prevention (Shaw, 1930; Shaw and McKay, 1931; Thrasher, 1927, 1936). Prevention programs typically attempt to prevent youth from joining gangs, but might also seek to interrupt gang formation. A variety of strategies have been employed to prevent youth involvement in gangs, including community organization, improving conditions for youth, early childhood programs, school-based programs, and local clubs and afterschool programs.

Community Organization

The Chicago Area Project (CAP) (Sorrentino, 1959; Sorrentino and Whittaker, 1994), created in 1934, was designed to implement "social disorganization" theories suggesting that community organization could be a major tool for reducing crime and gang problems. CAP was designed to involve local community groups in improving neighborhood conditions, such as the lack of supervised recreation and afterschool programs, that were believed to foster the formation of youth gangs.

CAP was the first program to initiate use of detached workers. Program activities included recreation, community self-renewal, mediation, and advocacy before government agencies and staff, especially school, probation, and parole officials (Schlossman and Sedlak, 1983). Claims of CAP's success continue to be publicized despite the absence of empirical evaluation results. The program is still operating, a clear indication of its perceived value among Chicago officials and community groups.

Another community-based gang program that, like CAP, relies on indigenous community organizations was established much later. The House of Umoja began operating in Philadelphia during the 1970's as a unique grassroots program initiated by community residents David and Falaka Fattah (National Center for Neighborhood Enterprise, 1999; see also Woodson, 1981, 1986, 1998). Using their own resources and their home as a base of operations, they created this family-centered community institution that effectively mediated gang conflicts and came to serve as a source of counsel and individual development for neighborhood gang and nongang youth. The family model "provides a sense of belonging, identity, and self-worth that was previously sought through gang membership" (National Center for Neighborhood Enterprise, 1999:59). Through reparenting[2] and providing role models, the House of Umoja has "successfully transformed more than five hundred frightened, frustrated, and alienated young minority males into self-assured, competent, concerned, and productive citizens" (National Center for Neighborhood Enterprise, 1999:16). The National Center for Neighborhood Enterprise (NCNE) has identified eight characteristics associated with the House of Umoja's success (National Center for Neighborhood Enterprise, 1999):

◆ A family-centered organization that acts as youth's primary human support system and is based on a participatory model of decisionmaking.

◆ A process of socialization in which at-risk youth develop strong, healthy identities and may even earn the name Fattah, after the House of Umoja's initiators.

◆ The Adella, a mechanism for conflict resolution and problem solving that requires full participation of all members.

◆ Individual learning to organize personal time and space.

◆ An emphasis on the importance of work and a redefinition of the meaning of work associated with virtue.

◆ An emphasis on service to others.

_____

[2] Reparenting involves adults who act as parents, giving youth unconditional love, clear standards of behavior, and constant availability.

◆ A spiritual or ideological context expressed in common familial rituals.

◆ Leadership training and development.

Improving Conditions and Creating Opportunities

Efforts to prevent youth gang involvement have long been part of community-based youth service programs. Albuquerque's Youth Development, Inc. (YDI), provides comprehensive services for at-risk youth and others involved in the juvenile justice system (Carnegie Council on Adolescent Development, 1994). YDI's Gang Prevention and Intervention Program is directed toward preventing initial gang involvement among younger teenagers and providing constructive, nonviolent activities for current gang members. In a structured 7-week program, gang members become involved in community service, learn nonviolent conflict resolution skills, obtain employment and legal assistance, and receive counseling with family members.

Inner-City Games (ICG) is another urban program that provides alternatives to gang life (Gates, 1998). Licensed by the National Inner-City Games Foundation and chaired by Arnold Schwarzenegger, ICG provides opportunities for inner-city youth to participate in athletic, educational, cultural, and community-enrichment programs. The program enables youth to build confidence and self-esteem and encourages them to say "no" to gangs, drugs, and violence and "yes" to hope, learning, and life. Originally assisting youth only in East Los Angeles, ICG now operates in 12 cities, serving more than 1 million young people.

Other programs for improving economic conditions and individual opportunities in gang-ridden neighborhoods include community reconstruction (Eisenhower Foundation, 1990), Empowerment Zones (revitalizing communities through economic and social services), and Enterprise Communities (promoting physical and human development). Supported by the U.S. Department of Housing and Urban Development (HUD), Empowerment Zones and Enterprise Communities are large-scale programs that seek to reconstruct selected inner-city areas (Office of Juvenile Justice and Delinquency Prevention, 1995b).

The following are descriptions of three programs designed to prevent gang problems in particularly low-income areas and public housing projects:

◆ **The Beethoven Project** in Chicago's Robert Taylor Homes (Center for Successful Child Development, 1993) was designed to ensure a head start for mothers and their infants by providing a variety of health and social services, mainly through a family drop-in center (Short, 1996).

◆ **The Neutral Zone** (Thurman et al., 1996), a recreation/services facility operating in several communities in the State of Washington, offers high-risk youth, many of whom may be involved in gangs, a safe alternative to being out on the streets late at night.

◆ **The Community Outreach Program** (Kodluboy and Evenrud, 1993), a St. Paul, MN, Police Department program, includes prompt diversion of first-time offenders and school liaison work in the city's Southeast Asian community, which has become affected by gangs.

The neighborhood block watch also appears to be a useful community crime prevention technique for public housing projects and other neighborhoods (Lindsay and McGillis, 1986; Rosenbaum, Lewis, and Grant, 1986). Other community-based initiatives that help prevent gang involvement include manhood development (culturally specific mentoring that matches youth with adult role models) (Watts, 1991), neighborhood youth centers (e.g., Nuestro Centro, see Office of Juvenile Justice and Delinquency Prevention, 1995a), the use of gang members in outreach efforts (e.g., Comin' Up, City of Fort Worth, TX, 1996; see Curry, 1995), and the Community Reclamation Project (1990), which demonstrated how to establish an ongoing, integrated network of community-based organizations, agencies, and citizens that would effectively combat emerging gang problems.

Early Childhood Programs

Battin-Pearson and colleagues (1999:20) concluded that "once in a gang, those youths who are most behaviorally and socially maladjusted in childhood are most likely to remain in a gang for multiple years." The Seattle study (Hill et al., 1999) identified a variety of childhood risk factors that, if present between the ages of 10 and 12, are predictive of gang membership during adolescence (see table 2). Clearly, prevention efforts should begin early.

The Montreal Preventive Treatment Program (Tremblay et al., 1996) illustrates how multiple-component prevention programs can effectively address early childhood risk factors for gang involvement. This program was designed to prevent antisocial behavior among boys of low socioeconomic status who displayed disruptive problem behavior in kindergarten. By incorporating an approach focused on risk and protective factors, it demonstrated that a combination of parent training and childhood skills development can steer antisocial children away from gangs. Parent training was combined with individual social skills training for boys ages 7 to 9. Parents received an average of 17 training sessions that focused on monitoring their children's behavior, giving positive reinforcement for prosocial behavior, using punishment effectively, and managing family crises. The boys received 19 training sessions to improve prosocial skills and self-control. The training was implemented in small groups containing both disruptive and nondisruptive boys and used coaching, peer modeling, self-instruction, reinforcement contingencies, and role-playing to build skills. An evaluation of the program showed both short- and long-term gains, including less delinquency, substance use, and gang involvement at age 15 (Tremblay et al., 1996).

Other early childhood development programs combined with parent training have proven effective in preventing involvement in delinquency and crime into early adulthood, although they were not tested for the prevention of gang involvement. The High/Scope Perry Preschool Project (Schweinhart, Barnes, and Weikart, 1993) and the Syracuse University Family Development Research Project (Lally, Mangione, and Honig, 1988) have been shown to be effective in reducing severe and chronic delinquency in long-term followups, although High/Scope was far more cost effective (Aos et al., 1999). High/Scope sought to prevent school failure in poor, African American 3- and 4-year-olds. Children were enrolled in preschool, and their teachers conducted home visits to inform parents of the child's activities and to promote parental involvement in his or her educational experience.

Table 2. Risk Factors at Ages 10–12 for Subsequent Gang Membership, Seattle, WA

Potential Childhood Risk Factor	Membership Prevalence*	Odds Ratio for Those at High Risk
Neighborhood		
Availability of marijuana	30%	3.6
Neighborhood youth in trouble	26	3.0
Low neighborhood attachment	20	1.5
Family		
Poverty (low household income)	23%	2.1
One parent in home	21	2.4
One parent and other adults in home	25	3.0
No parents in home	24	2.9
Parental alcohol intake	15	1.0
Sibling antisocial behavior	22	1.9
Poor family management	21	1.7
Parental proviolent attitudes	26	2.3
Low attachment to parents	20	1.5
School		
Low academic aspirations	20%	1.6
Low school commitment	21	1.8
Low school attachment	23	2.0
Low academic achievement in elementary school	28	3.1
Identified as learning disabled	36	3.6
Peer		
Association with peers who engage in problem behaviors	26%	2.0
Individual		
Low religious service attendance	15%	1.0
Antisocial beliefs	23	2.0
Respondent drinking	20	1.6
Respondent marijuana initiation	37	3.7
Violence	28	3.1
Personality/Individual Difference		
Externalizing	26%	2.6
Internalizing	19	1.4
Hyperactivity	21	1.7
Poor refusal skills	23	1.8

* For each risk factor, this column shows gang membership prevalence (the percentage of youth joining a gang) among youth who had scored in the worst quarter on the risk factor at ages 10–12.
Source: Hill et al., 1999.

In addition, parental support and information exchange services were made available. The Syracuse University project delivered services (including educational, nutritional, health, safety, and human service resources) to pregnant mothers and to mothers with children who had not yet reached elementary school (children under age 5). Childcare was provided while trained home visitors made weekly visits.

School-Based Programs

Gang presence in schools is increasing. Students bring preexisting gang conflicts to the school setting, and new conflicts are created when opposing gang members come into contact with one another. Two nationwide student surveys show that between 1989 and 1995, the proportion of students reporting that street gangs were present in their schools nearly doubled (Chandler et al., 1998). More than a third (37 percent) reported gang presence in their schools in 1995 (Howell and Lynch, in press).

Goldstein and Kodluboy (1998) suggest that programs in school settings must, at a minimum, include three types of strategies:

◆ In-school safety and control procedures (see also Trump, 1998).

◆ In-school enrichment procedures that make the school experience more meaningful, effective, and enjoyable (see also Howell and Hawkins, 1998).

◆ Formal links to community-based programs.

Goldstein and Kodluboy (1998) also assert that gang initiatives in schools should be research based, data driven, and outcome focused. A comprehensive assessment of school-related gang problems and school safety issues should be made in conjunction with an assessment of risk factors for gang involvement and delinquency in the surrounding community. Communities should not move into the program development stage before these important steps are completed, because a sound base of research and data are needed for effective program development. Kodluboy and Evenrud (1993) suggest that school-focused gang programs be developed in collaboration with community agencies. These programs should:

◆ Share the common mission and objectives of the school and school district.

Examples of School-Based Programs

Goldstein and Kodluboy (1998) describe a number of programs with which schools might develop links:

◆ Academy High School (Patterson, NJ).

◆ Big Brothers/Big Sisters of America (New Jersey's School-Based Youth Services Program).

◆ Broader Urban Involvement and Leadership Development (Chicago, IL).

◆ The City of Fort Worth's Comin' Up Program (Boys & Girls Clubs of America).

◆ Collaborative Intensive Community Treatment Program (Erie, PA).

◆ Communities In Schools (Alexandria, VA).

◆ El Puente ("The Bridge," Brooklyn, NY).

◆ Gang Peace/First (Roxbury, MA).

◆ Golden Eagles (Phillips Community American Indian Center, Minneapolis, MN).

◆ Gulf Coast Trades Center (New Waverly, TX).

◆ The Neutral Zone (Mountainlake Terrace, WA).

◆ Project RAISE (Baltimore, MD).

◆ Project Save-A-Youth (Anaheim, CA).

◆ Youth Works (Louisville, KY).

- Be public and accountable.

- Be based on the established standards of the profession or social service agency involved.

- Have specific, written projected outcomes.

- Have reasonable timelines for attaining the projected outcomes and meeting commitments.

- Monitor progress toward individual agency objectives, using simple, direct measures.

- Be subject to external review.

- Demonstrate social validity through broad-based community involvement of all interested parties, such as businesses, neighborhood representatives, and others.

- Be free of cultural bias and consistent with prevailing prosocial community goals and norms.

Coordinated efforts that link school, police, probation, and other agencies also need to be attentive to restrictions on information sharing and exceptions to those restrictions under the Family Educational Rights and Privacy Act (20 U.S.C. § 1232g). This Federal law governs the disclosure of information from education records.[3]

The following paragraphs describe a variety of promising school-based gang prevention programs.

PASSPORT. A unique program designed to protect children from gangs, Parents and Schools Succeeding in Providing Organized Routes to Travel (PASSPORT) is a joint effort of the Visalia, CA, school district, the police department, parents, and community organizations (Arnette and Walsleben, 1998). Students use supervised routes when traveling to and from school in high-crime or gang-oriented areas. Parents are provided with maps designating these recommended routes. Police routinely patrol—and school administrators and the safe school coordinator also monitor and walk—PASSPORT communities

---

[3] *Sharing Information: A Guide to the Family Educational Rights and Privacy Act and Participation in Juvenile Justice Programs* (Medaris, Campbell, and James, 1997), a detailed guide to the Act, assists schools and other agencies in developing records systems and establishing information-sharing protocols. It is available free from the Juvenile Justice Clearinghouse (800–638–8736).

and routes. Parent volunteers stand in front of their homes and "just watch" during specified hours. Fights, intimidating behaviors, and unsafe activities are immediately reported to the nearest school or to other appropriate agencies. Media publicity about PASSPORT encourages all citizens to watch over schoolchildren to ensure their safe passage to and from school. The program depends on cooperative volunteer efforts. Actual dollar costs are minimal.

Antibullying programs. Bullying at school may be a contributor to joining gangs. The need for protection is a major reason gang members cite for joining a gang (Decker and Van Winkle, 1996). Students who report the presence of gangs and weapons in school are about twice as likely to report having been victims of a violent crime (e.g., physical attack, robbery, or bullying) (Chandler et al., 1998). Antibullying school programs may have the added benefit of preventing gang victimization. Olweus (1992) conducted a successful school antibullying program in Bergen, Norway, that consisted of four program components:

- A booklet for school personnel was distributed to all Bergen comprehensive schools (grades 1 to 9). It described bully/victim problems, provided suggestions about what teachers and the school could do to counteract and prevent such problems, and dispelled myths about the nature and causes of bullying.

- An information packet was distributed to all families in Bergen with school-age children. It contained information on bullying and advice for parents on how to address it.

- A videocassette that depicted episodes from the daily lives of two early adolescent bullying victims was made available for purchase or rent at a subsidized price.

- A brief anonymous questionnaire about bullying problems was administered to students in all comprehensive schools, the results of which were used to inform school and family interventions.

An evaluation of the Bergen program showed that the prevalence of bullying victims decreased substantially (Olweus, 1991, 1992). In 1992, Smith and Sharp (1994) implemented a similar program for schools in Sheffield, England. The core program involved establishing an antibullying policy for the entire school, increasing awareness, and clearly defining roles and responsibilities of teachers and students, so that everyone knew what bullying was and what they should do about it. Evaluation proved the program to be successful in reducing bullying among young children; the program had relatively small effects on older children. However, an adaptation of the Olweus model for use in rural middle schools in South Carolina did not significantly decrease the rate of bullying (Melton et al., 1998).

Se Puede. The Se Puede ("You Can") program in San Juan, TX, operates in a tricity area (Alamo, Pharr, and San Juan) that has about 5,000 gang members (Office of Juvenile Justice and Delinquency Prevention, 1999). It seeks to prevent at-risk middle school youth from becoming involved with gangs, gun violence, and drugs and to improve their academic performance by providing:

◆ Individual and group counseling.

◆ Positive alternatives and role models in a voluntary 1-year program.

◆ A curriculum component, Project Hart, that combines principles and skills for preventing substance abuse and violence in weekly culturally sensitive lessons.

◆ Monthly weekend camping experiences in which small groups of students learn survival skills and develop relationships with mentors.

An evaluation of the Se Peude program showed a decrease in gang involvement among participating students despite an increase in the number of gangs in the tricity area during the program period. In addition, Se Puede program participants showed a decrease on several measures of crime involvement and improved individual skills and school performance (Office of Juvenile Justice and Delinquency Prevention, 1999).

Gang Resistance Is Paramount. In an attempt to curb gang membership and discourage future gang involvement, the city of Paramount, CA, initiated the Gang Resistance Is Paramount (G.R.I.P.) program (Arnette and Walsleben, 1998). The program in-

cludes three major components. The first involves neighborhood meetings that provide parents with support, assistance, and resources as they try to prevent their children from joining gangs. The second component comprises a 15-week course for fifth grade students and a 10-week course for second grade students. The lessons deal with graffiti, peer pressure, tattoos, the impact of gang activity on family members, drug abuse, and alternative activities and opportunities. Finally, a school-based followup program is implemented at the ninth grade level to reinforce what children learned in the elementary grades. The program is designed to build self-esteem and also focuses on the consequences of a criminal lifestyle, the benefits of higher education, and future career opportunities. Three studies conducted by Paramount's Community Services and Recreation department show significant program effects in terms of youth developing negative attitudes toward gangs and staying out of them. In a long-term followup, 96 percent of more than 3,000 program participants were not identified as gang members in police records (Arnette and Walsleben, 1998).

Gang Resistance Education and Training Program. Discouraging children and young adolescents from joining gangs may be the most cost-effective approach to reducing serious youth and adult gang crime (National Drug Intelligence Center, 1994). Evaluation of the Bureau of Alcohol, Tobacco and Firearms' (ATF's) Gang Resistance Education and Training (G.R.E.A.T.) Program curriculum has shown positive preliminary results in this regard (Esbensen and Osgood, 1997). G.R.E.A.T. is "built on the strategy of delivering a simple, low-intensity program to as large a population as possible" (Esbensen and Osgood, 1999:218). The G.R.E.A.T. curriculum is administered in a school-based program in which uniformed law enforcement officers teach a 9-week course to middle school students (Esbensen and Osgood, 1997, 1999; Lesce, 1993). The curriculum includes the following components:

◆ Introduction—students are introduced to G.R.E.A.T. and the presenting officer.

◆ Crime/Victims and Your Rights—students learn about crimes, their victims, and their impact on the school and neighborhood.

◆ Cultural Sensitivity/Prejudice—students are taught how cultural differences affect their school and neighborhood.

◆ Conflict Resolution—students learn how to create an atmosphere of understanding that will enable all parties to better address interpersonal problems and work together on solutions.

◆ Meeting Basic Needs—students are taught how to satisfy their basic social needs without joining a gang.

◆ Drugs/Neighborhoods—students learn how drugs affect their school and neighborhood.

◆ Responsibility—students learn about the diverse responsibilities of people in their school and neighborhood.

◆ Goal Setting—students are taught the need for personal goal setting and ways to establish short- and long-term goals.

In followup surveys conducted between 12 and 18 months after completion of the program, students reported lower levels than before of gang affiliation and delinquency, including drug use, minor offending, property crimes, and crimes against persons (Esbensen and Osgood, 1997, 1999). Compared with the control group, the treatment group reported fewer delinquent friends, more positive attitudes toward the police, more negative attitudes about gangs, more friends involved in prosocial activities, greater commitment to peers promoting prosocial behavior, higher self-esteem, more commitment to success at school, higher levels of attachment to both mothers and fathers, and less likelihood of acting impulsively. The authors of the study cautioned that the positive program results were modest: "Clearly, this program is not a 'silver bullet' or a panacea for gang violence" (Esbensen and Osgood, 1999:217). A longitudinal evaluation that will assess long-term effects of the program is under way. Because of the limited positive effects, ATF is redesigning the G.R.E.A.T. curriculum to make it more effective.

The effectiveness of prevention curriculums might be enhanced by combining them with an afterschool program such as Nuestro Centro (a community-run youth center that provides an afterschool program for youth affected by drugs, gangs, and delinquency) (Office of Juvenile Justice and Delinquency Prevention, 1995a) or an antibullying program (Olweus, 1992). School-based programs should include a gang intervention component because gang-related crime has been shown to escalate and peak earlier in the school day than other violent juvenile crime (Wiebe, Meeker, and Vila, in press).

Evaluation of school-based programs. An OJJDP-funded National Study of School-Based Gang Prevention and Intervention Programs is in progress. It builds on a large-scale National Study of Delinquency Prevention in Schools (Gottfredson and Gottfredson, 1996). The OJJDP study makes use of a nationally representative sample of 1,287 schools surveyed in the national prevention study. Two-thirds of the schools (66 percent) provided information on gang prevention and intervention programs in categories supplied by the researchers (e.g., prevention curriculum, mentoring, tutoring) (Gottfredson and Gottfredson, 1999). School "activity coordinators" were asked for more detailed information on school gang programs. Current school programs will be compared with "best practices." Teachers and students also were surveyed to obtain reports of problem behavior and participation in gang prevention and intervention programs. These data are being analyzed and reports are forthcoming. The Centers for Disease Control and Prevention (CDC) is supporting the implementation and evaluation of 13 violence prevention programs, many of which are based in school and some of which address gang violence (Powell and Hawkins, 1996).

Afterschool Activities

Gang Prevention Through Targeted Outreach, operated by Boys & Girls Clubs of America (BGCA), is a communitywide gang prevention program that incorporates four objectives: community mobilization, recruitment, mainstreaming/programming, and case management.

Local implementation of this program, which has been described as a promising prevention initiative (Thornberry and Burch, 1997), begins with mobilizing community leaders and club staff, who discuss local gang issues and clarify their roles as they design a strategy to prevent gangs and offer youth alternatives to the gang lifestyle. Police departments, schools, social service agencies, and community organizations recruit at-risk youth into club programs in a nonstigmatizing way through direct outreach efforts and a referral network that links local clubs with courts. In the Boys & Girls Club, youth participate in programs based on their individual interests and needs. Programs are offered in five core areas: character and leadership development; education and career development; health and life skills; the arts; and sports, fitness, and recreation.

Case management is an integral part of the program. Staff document monthly progress on specific goals in the following areas: academic performance, involvement in the juvenile justice system, program participation, and family involvement.

In the early 1990's, an initial evaluation reported that once enrolled in Boys & Girls Clubs of America, as many as 48 percent of the youth showed improvement in the academic arena (Feyerherm, Pope, and Lovell, 1992). Specifically, more than 33 percent of the youth showed improved grades, and as many as 33 percent had better school attendance. OJJDP is currently funding an outcome evaluation of the Gang Prevention Through Targeted Outreach strategy, which will be completed in 2000.

The prevention component of Broader Urban Involvement and Leadership Development (BUILD) (Brewer et al., 1995; Ribisl and Davidson, 1993), developed in the mid-1980's and still operating, consists of a gang prevention curriculum and an after-school program. Thompson and Jason's (1988) evaluation of the program showed that youth in BUILD were less likely to join a gang than youth in the comparison group, but the difference was only marginally statistically significant. The evaluation was limited by a short-term followup period and a relatively small sample size.

Implications of Risk and Protective Factors

Youth gang involvement is preventable. For reasons that are not well understood, gangs have become a very popular adolescent peer group, one of many peer groups that youth try out during their adoles-

cent years (Fleisher, 1998). Most adolescents who join a gang do not remain long—at least in newer gang problem cities. Studies in Denver, CO; Rochester, NY; and Seattle, WA (Thornberry, 1998), showed that from one-half to two-thirds stayed in a gang for 1 year or less; one-third or more belonged for multiple years.

These longitudinal studies of large samples of urban adolescents have examined risk factors for gang membership (see Hill et al., 1999, for a summary).[4] Risk factors for multiple-year membership have been examined in the Seattle study. In the Rochester study, part of the OJJDP-funded Program of Research on the Causes and Correlates of Delinquency, Bjerregaard and Smith (1993) found that similar factors predicted gang membership among both males and females, including delinquent peers and early sexual activity.[5] In Denver, another site in the Causes and Correlates program, Esbensen and colleagues (1993) found that higher commitment to delinquent peers, lower commitment to positive peers, more negative labeling by teachers, and higher peer tolerance for criminal activity were risk factors for gang membership.

In the Seattle study, which was supported by OJJDP and several other organizations, Hill and colleagues (1999) examined risk factors in childhood (ages 10–12) for adolescent gang membership (age 13 and beyond) (see table 2, page 8). They found that risk factors span all major risk factor domains: community, family, school, peer group, and individual characteristics. The most important community factor is growing up in neighborhoods in which drugs are readily available. Several family variables are important: family instability, extreme economic deprivation, low attachment to the mother, family management problems,

---

[4] Howell (1998b) reviewed risk factors for gang membership that have been identified in cross-sectional studies. These studies are not as reliable as longitudinal studies for identifying risk factors because cross-sectional studies measure both risk factors and outcomes in the same time period; thus, a predictor could well be an outcome of gang involvement.

[5] Gang prevention programs should target females in addition to males. Analyses of data collected in the National Evaluation of the G.R.E.A.T. curriculum show that females are well-represented in gangs and that the overwhelming majority of youth gangs have female members (Deschenes and Esbensen, 1999; Esbensen and Deschenes, 1998; Esbensen, Deschenes, and Winfree, 1999; Esbensen and Winfree, 1998).

family conflict, parent proviolent attitudes, and sibling antisocial behavior. Numerous school factors are very important, including low educational aspiration, low commitment and attachment to school, high levels of antisocial behavior, low achievement test scores, identification as being learning disabled, and low grades. The most important peer group factor is associating with "bad" peers; conversely, high attachment to conventional peers decreases the probability of joining gangs. Individual risk factors include early involvement in antisocial behavior, hyperactivity, externalizing behaviors, alcohol consumption, lack of social competence, and early sexual activity. This study also found that the odds of joining a gang increase greatly when multiple risk factors are present in childhood.

Battin-Pearson and colleagues (1999) examined risk factors for sustained (multiple-year) gang membership, comparing these with predictors or risk factors for nonmembership and transitory (single-year) membership. The strongest predictors of sustained membership versus nonmembership are having learning disabilities; interacting with antisocial peers and not much with prosocial peers; and exhibiting low social competence, low academic achievement, early antisocial behavior, early violence, early marijuana use, high internalization, and high externalizing behavior. The strongest predictors of sustained membership versus single-year membership are high interaction with antisocial peers and low interaction with prosocial peers, early antisocial behavior, high internalization, and high externalizing behavior. A survey designed to help identify risk factors for gang membership will be available from the National Youth Gang Center.[6]

Few studies have addressed protective (resilience) factors that buffer children and adolescents from gang involvement. Thus, research is needed in this area. Although some protective factors are the converse of risk factors (e.g., early academic achievement, the antithesis of low school performance, can be expected to protect children from gang involvement), other protective factors may reside in mental and social development processes that are not linked to risk factors (Rutter, Giller, and Hagell, 1998). Maxson and colleagues (1998) suggest several protective factors that might buffer adolescents from gang involvement (e.g., counseling for youth who experience multiple stressful events).[7]

One study examined risk factors for gang membership among a sample of Asian adolescents in Westminster, CA (Wyrick, 2000), and also identified possible protective factors against gang involvement. Surprisingly, this study found that Vietnamese youth who reject their Asian identity and find it difficult to adopt an American identity are not more likely than other Vietnamese youth to join gangs. Rather, researchers identified two main factors that predict Vietnamese youth gang involvement: progang attitudes and exposure to gangs in the neighborhood. Four predictors were found to influence the development of progang attitudes: negative school attitude, family conflict, poor social integration (i.e., a generalized sense of alienation), and perceived benefits of gang membership. As for protective factors, the researchers suggested that while services focusing solely on cultural identity issues may have benefits, they will not be effective in preventing or reducing gang involvement by Vietnamese youth. Instead, services should focus on improving youth attitudes about school, reducing feelings of alienation, and modifying perceptions that gangs are beneficial to their members. Furthermore, the researchers suggested that services might prevent gang involvement if they address family conflict and buffer the influences of neighborhood gangs (Wyrick, 2000).

Intervention Programs

Intervention programs seek to reduce the criminal activities of gangs by coaxing youth away from gangs and reducing criminality among gang members. These programs, examples of which follow, provide alternative opportunities for youth and apply rehabilitation measures.

---

[6] For more information, call the Institute for Intergovernmental Research's National Youth Gang Center at 800–446–0912.

[7] This was a cross-sectional study. Longitudinal research designs are stronger for determining protective factors that serve as buffers from gang involvement at a later point in adolescence.

Detached Worker Programs

A significant shift in youth gang program approaches, from prevention by means of community organization to interventions relying almost exclusively on detached workers, occurred in the 1940's with the establishment of the New York City Youth Board (1960). Created to combat the city's growing number of fighting gangs, this city-run program relied on detached workers to transform youth gangs from fighting groups into pro-social ones. Most of the transformation was to be accomplished in the streets where gangs met, played, and hung out. Worker activities included securing health care for gang members, providing employment counseling, doing advocacy work with the police and courts, and taking almost any other action that might transform gang values or lure juveniles away from them (Geis, 1965). Although the program was never evaluated, it served as a forerunner of later detached worker programs.

The Boston detached worker program, a community-wide project, consisted of three major program components: community organization, family service, and gang work. For 3 years, staff in the Midcity Project—established in the Roxbury section of Boston in 1954—worked with 400 members of 21 street corner gangs. In perhaps the most rigorous gang program evaluation ever conducted (Miller, 1962), the project proved to be ineffective.

Evaluation of a California detached worker program brought into even more serious question the value of this approach (Klein, 1971, 1995a). The Group Guidance Project, begun in the 1940's by the Los Angeles Probation Department, employed group guidance by street workers in an attempt to intervene in the emergence of African American gangs in South Central Los Angeles. Group activities, including weekly club meetings, sports activities, tutoring, individual counseling, and advocacy with community agencies and organizations, were designed to reunite gang members with their community institutions. Klein (1995a:145) concluded that "increased group programming leads to increased cohesiveness (in both gang growth and gang 'tightness'), and increased cohesiveness leads to increased gang crime." Based on these results, Klein has repeatedly warned practitioners against any activities that might contribute to gang cohesion, because these might increase gang delinquency (Klein, 1995a).

Warning Signs

Identifying bona fide gangs is a difficult task. It is important for communities to recognize the warning signs of a gang problem. Trump (1998) lists the following gang identifiers for use by schools:

- ◆ **Graffiti.** Unusual signs, symbols, or writing on walls, notebooks, class assignments, or gang "literature" books.

- ◆ **Colors.** Obvious or subtle colors of clothing, a particular clothing brand, bandannas, jewelry, or haircuts.

- ◆ **Tattoos.** Symbols on the body.

- ◆ **Initiations.** Suspicious bruises, wounds, or injuries resulting from a "jumping in." Gang initiations have taken place in school restrooms, gyms, locker rooms, playgrounds, and even hallways.

- ◆ **Hand signs.** Unusual hand signals or handshakes.

- ◆ **Language.** Uncommon terms or phrases.

- ◆ **Behavior.** Sudden changes in behavior or secret meetings.

It is important to consider multiple factors in assessing whether youth groups are bona fide gangs. Other researchers and organizations have developed similar indicators that can be used in making a determination of gang formation (Curry and Decker, 1998; National Drug Intelligence Center, 1995).

The Ladino Hills Project, created in East Los Angeles in 1967, was an experiment Klein (1968) designed to test his hypothesis that if gang cohesiveness could be reduced through nongroup (i.e., individual) interventions, then gang delinquency would be reduced. Interventions included job training, tutoring, recreation in established agencies, and individual therapy. Klein's evaluation showed that gang cohesiveness was reduced by about 40 percent, and an overall reduction of 35 percent in gang member arrests was observed, although this was attributed mainly to fewer gang members. However, several years later, the gang reassumed its preproject character. Klein (1995a:147) concluded that "we had affected the [gang members] but not their community. The lesson is both obvious and important. Gangs are byproducts of their communities: They cannot long be controlled by attacks on symptoms alone; community structure and capacity must also be targeted."

Although researchers disagree about the effectiveness of detached worker programs (Bursik and Grasmick, 1993; Goldstein and Glick, 1994), it must be concluded that, as a singular intervention, detached workers have not conclusively produced positive results. Numerous reasons have been offered to account for the lack of effectiveness of this strategy. Klein (1971; see also Spergel, 1966) suggested that it was unclear whether these programs were designed to control gangs, treat gang members' personality problems, provide access to social and cultural opportunities, transform values, or prevent delinquency. Conflicting program objectives made evaluation difficult.

Crisis Intervention

In the next "era" of youth gang programming, detached workers were put in vehicles and sent to "hotspots" of gang activity. Philadelphia's Crisis Intervention Network (CIN), established in 1974, pioneered the assignment of gang workers to work in specific areas rather than with specific gangs. They were to patrol hotspots in radio-dispatched cars, attempting to defuse potentially violent situations. Although CIN was not evaluated, it was declared a success by CIN officials, a claim that has been subject to challenge (Klein, 1995a; Needle and Stapleton, 1983; Spergel, 1995).

Despite doubts about the success of Philadelphia's CIN, the program was transplanted to Los Angeles (beginning in 1980–81) and named the Community Youth Gang Services (CYGS) program. Like CIN, CYGS used suppression tactics (e.g., dispatching patrol teams in specially marked cars), social intervention efforts, group programming and outings for gang members, and truce meetings (Klein, 1995a). According to Klein, implementation of the program was not successful.

Spergel (1986) evaluated the Crisis Intervention Services Project (see also Ribisl and Davidson, 1993), which was implemented in the mid-1980's in a gang-ridden section of Chicago. Spergel (1995:255) described the program as a "mixed social intervention or crisis intervention approach, with strong deterrent and community involvement characteristics." Staff patrolled areas where gang violence was likely to erupt during evening and late-night hours, attempting to mediate conflicts. Intensive counseling was provided to gang youth referred by the juvenile court and to their families. Local neighborhood groups were mobilized and involved in the project. Spergel's evaluation (1986) showed that the program appeared to reduce the most serious and violent crimes, but not overall crime levels. Nevertheless, these were the most encouraging gang intervention results up to that time.

Crisis intervention programming as a singular approach using detached workers in an attempt to defuse gang conflicts does not have a stellar performance record. Spergel (1995) contended that a detached worker strategy by itself is inadequate to deal with complex challenges such as remedial education, job preparation and development, and community issues. Thus, the detached worker concept has been expanded over the past 30 years to incorporate other roles (Spergel and Curry, 1990). Most recently, in the Little Village Gang Violence Reduction Program, detached workers were redefined as "community youth workers," who "not only had to develop new quasi-professional skills related to referrals of gang youths to agency services or job placement, but [who] also had to learn to collaborate with police and probation officers in such a way that gang conflict was prevented or at least controlled" (Spergel and Grossman, 1997:462). This broader role appeared

Boys & Girls Clubs

In addition to the Gang Prevention Through Targeted Outreach program described on pages 12–13, Boys & Girls Clubs of America supports another youth gang program. Comin' Up, located in Fort Worth, TX, is a youth gang intervention program developed out of training provided by Boys & Girls Clubs (Boys & Girls Clubs of Greater Fort Worth, 1996; City of Fort Worth, 1996) and is based on a Boys & Girls Clubs' gang intervention strategy. All program youth are identified gang members. Needs assessments are made on all referrals by a team comprising project staff, school officials, parents, police, probation officers, and others. In addition to providing alternatives to gang life (especially education and employment) and providing life-skills development, the program works to establish truces among rival gangs and to reduce the incidence of gang violence. One of the program's unique features is the employment of successful clients as outreach workers. Criminal arrest data reported to the Federal Bureau of Investigation (FBI) indicate a significant decrease in violence in the area served by the project (Parks and Community Services Department, 1997). The program has not yet received an independent evaluation.

Improving Conditions

Homeboy Industries and Jobs for a Future—grassroots projects supported by the Dolores Mission in Boyle Heights, Los Angeles, CA (Gaouette, 1997)—provide alternatives to gang life for gang members: jobs that can give them an escape from gangs. Jobs for a Future places some 200 gang members in jobs in the community each year. Homeboy Industries merchandises T-shirts and silkscreens and operates Homeboy Bakeries, which sells baked bread to a commercial baker. Both enterprises successfully employ rival gang members. Proceeds from these ventures fund a daycare center, a homeless shelter, an alternative school for gang members, and a tattoo-removal service.

Providing jobs appears to be an effective intervention. In a survey of incarcerated adolescent and adult gang members across the country, Houston (1996) found that gang members viewed job training and jobs positively. Huff's (1998) study revealed that many gang members and nongang at-risk youth who sell drugs would give up selling for reasonable wages (less than $15 per hour), and many indicated that "they would accept far lower wages—not much more than is currently being paid in fast-food restaurants—if they could obtain a sufficient number of hours per week" (Huff, 1998:7). NCNE (1999:62) contends that "the belief that young people will not accept an entry-level job is a false and debilitating myth." Moore and Vigil (1993:43) reported that job programs in East Los Angeles gang areas that were provided in the 1960's through the war on poverty "without question" reduced gang violence. Once the programs were dismantled, gang violence increased. In his Kansas City study of "dead-end" gang members, Fleisher (1998:214) concluded that the "unlawful-to-lawful shift in income production . . . results in less crime and less serious crime." This conclusion is supported by a detailed review of programs for serious and violent juvenile offenders. Lipsey and Wilson (1998) found that paid employment reduces recidivism among offenders who are not incarcerated.

Violence-Free Zones

NCNE has developed Violence-Free Zones, a grassroots community intervention for youth and gang-related violence. The Violence-Free Zone model is based on the premise that the breakdown of the family structure is a key risk factor for gang involvement and a major contributor to destructive behavior. In many cases, gang members come from fatherless homes in which mothers struggle to meet the economic and individual needs of their children. Consequently, they find it difficult to provide the necessary guidance. Violence-Free Zone implementers fill this void, taking on the role of mentor and engaging in reparenting. Job training and work opportunities also are provided for youth's social, personal, and economic development to help them make the transition from gang life and criminality to violence-free lives and productive citizenship. Successful youth are given the opportunity to collaborate with youth in other communities and cities to develop and expand Violence-Free Zones.

to contribute significantly to an overall coordinated program approach (see pages 37–38 for further information on this project).

Social Intervention

Fleisher's (1998) study of the two most notorious gangs in Kansas City, MO (the Fremont Hustlers and Northeast Gangsters), provided the basis for his proposed program solution for gang-involved youth: if gang members can be shifted from unlawful to lawful income production, they will eventually experience an underlying moral shift in lifestyle orientations.

> Gang life is predicated on immediate economic gain from drug and other crime profits and social gain from the agency of rulelessness. Mainstream life is oriented toward the future, and social and material gains are slower but steadier, more reliable, and less risky. . . . [S]uccessful gang intervention depends on offering gang kids the unlawful-to-lawful socioeconomic trade by showing them exactly what they have to gain. . . . The answer is simple: immediate material gain, including money, food, clothes, and shelter. Improvements these kids can see, touch and possess will pull them off the streets (Fleisher, 1998:214–215).

"Gangs like the Fremont Hustlers and Northeast Gangsters are monuments to economic failure in households, neighborhoods, and communities," but community development projects are needed that make sense to neighborhood residents (Fleisher, 1998:208).

Fleisher proposes a social intervention approach modeled after OJJDP's Comprehensive, Community-Wide Approach to Gang Prevention, Intervention, and Suppression model. He (1998:211) suggests that there is "a discontinuity between the actual problems in gang-affiliated adolescents' lives and the remedies offered by social and law enforcement agencies. Simply put, the local juvenile justice system doesn't give [gang] kids what they need . . . when they need it." Moreover, he argues, social service or law enforcement agencies "cannot intervene effectively in socioeconomic processes embedded in a family's transgenerational history." The program needs of gang girls are particularly acute. Fleisher therefore suggests creation of adult-supervised residential centers for adolescent girls who are affiliated with gangs. These centers would focus on three specific objectives: "(1) to shelter and protect girls; (2) to provide education, job training, and job placement; and (3) to ensure a healthy start for gang girls' children" (Fleisher, 1998:219; see pages 218–225 for detailed descriptions of how the centers could be designed to achieve these objectives). These residential centers should be located outside high-crime inner cities but close to high schools, community colleges, and jobs. Such decentralized centers would have advantages for gang youth over traditional centralized service delivery systems: "[C]entralized services are ineffective with gang kids, because they don't have cars to go downtown; they don't take buses; they don't go" (Fleisher, 1998:210).

This replicable model is based on the House of Umoja program and the success of similarly designed neighborhood initiatives in other cities (National Center for Neighborhood Enterprise, 1999). In Washington, DC, the faith-based Alliance for Concerned Men, a grassroots organization, was instrumental in establishing a Violence-Free Zone in the Benning Terrace public housing project with assistance from NCNE and the DC Housing Authority. Each of these three components contributed to the effort—NCNE provided technical assistance; the alliance carried out grassroots intervention in gang conflicts; and the Housing Authority provided job opportunities such as refurbishing the neighborhood, removing graffiti, and landscaping. Together they constitute the necessary structure for implementing a Violence-Free Zone. HUD and OJJDP are supporting the establishment of Violence-Free Zones in cities such as Dallas, TX; Indianapolis, IN; and Los Angeles, CA.

In 1998, NCNE convened representatives of successful grassroots initiatives to identify effective strategies and key elements of community-centered approaches. Entitled "best practices," these are described in detail in an NCNE (1999) publication, which also outlines practical steps in implementing the Violence-Free Zone model, under the following headings:

- Agents of effective youth intervention.

- Methods of intervention.

- Attitudes and premises of successful outreach.

- Collaborative efforts and sustainable youth intervention: the role of the public sector, private sector, and mutual support.

Gang Summits and Truces

Preventing gang wars by means of truces is an intervention that has not been systematically evaluated. Reports indicate that some truces have been successful but others have failed (Spergel, 1995). Gang homicides in Los Angeles were said to have dropped in 1994, presumably because of a truce between warring African American gangs that began in 1992 (Cotton, 1992). Klein (1995a) noted numerous instances in which adult-sponsored truce meetings backfired, reinforcing rivalries, increasing gang cohesion, and solidifying gang leadership.

Gang summits and truces negotiated by local residents may be more effective than those brought about in other ways. In the District of Columbia, members of the Alliance for Concerned Men negotiated a truce among warring gangs that had been terrorizing Benning Terrace. In January 1997, with the help of NCNE (1999), which assisted in strategic planning and provided a neutral meeting location, the alliance stepped in after a period of escalating violence. Six homicides had occurred in Benning Terrace in 1996. Following the alliance's intervention, there were no homicides from January 1997 to August 1998 (National Center for Neighborhood Enterprise, 1999).

Emergency Room Intervention and Victim Programs

The hospital emergency room is a promising arena for intervening in gang violence, including homicide.[8] Hutson and colleagues (1995) suggest that an emergency room intervention program for injured victims could help to break the cycle of gang violence. Others

---

[8] See Howell, 1998a:308–310, for a comprehensive approach to preventing and reducing gang homicide that integrates several program components.

have proposed counseling for victims of drive-by shootings to reduce the traumatic effects of victimization and discourage retaliation (Groves et al., 1993; Hutson, Anglin, and Pratts, 1994; Pynoos and Nader, 1988). One example of an emergency room program, the Partnership for a Safer Cleveland, provides gang recognition seminars for hospital emergency room staff. As a result, gang-involved youth are referred elsewhere for medical and psychological services (Walker and Schmidt, 1996).

Teens on Target (TNT), administered by Youth Alive!, a nonprofit agency in Oakland, CA, seeks to reduce youth injuries and death from gang-related and other gun violence through peer education, intervention, mentoring, and leadership development (Office of Juvenile Justice and Delinquency Prevention, 1999). TNT leaders—many of them violence victims—developed a training curriculum to address the relationship between violence and family contexts, guns, gangs, and drugs; the causes and effects of violence; and advocacy skills necessary to stop such violence. The leaders conduct student workshops, mediate conflicts between rival racial groups, and run a peer visitation program for hospitalized adolescents recovering from serious injuries to dissuade them and their friends from retaliation. A sister initiative operates in Los Angeles, CA. Together, the two TNT programs have won many awards for their work, including the California Peace Prize.

Intervention with victims of gang violence can also be accomplished outside hospital emergency rooms. The Child Development-Community Policing (CD–CP) model in New Haven, CT, is an excellent example (see Marans and Berkman, 1997). In this program, police refer victims of violent crimes, including victims of gang violence, to the CD–CP program for counseling. The Gang Victim Services Program, Orange County, CA, offers a full range of services and multilingual, multicultural support (Office for Victims of Crime, 1996). It also is important to protect victims and witnesses from gang intimidation (see Finn and Healey, 1996, for procedures and protections). Gang intimidation is but one problem that Miethe and McCorkle (1997a) found among many obstacles to effective prosecution of gang members in Las Vegas, NV.

Gang Members in Juvenile Detention and Correctional Facilities

Confinement in a juvenile correctional facility is a strong predictor of adult prison gang membership (Ralph et al., 1996). Prison gang members, in turn, contribute to the growth of youth gangs. In Chicago, prison gangs were said to exert considerable control over and have influence on street gangs (Decker, Bynum, and Weisel, 1998). "Prison gangs such as the Aryan Brotherhood, Mexican Mafia, and Texas Syndicate originated in prison and now have members on the street. Conversely, most street gangs now have members in prison" (Fleisher, 1995:131). In some cities, local gang activity is being orchestrated from the prisons (National Center for Neighborhood Enterprise, 1999). This development makes intervention in the resulting stronger "new breed of gangs" all the more difficult. Older gang members from juvenile correctional facilities and prisons who return to the street "align with neighborhood teenage gang members who are on the street, and form a larger, potentially more dangerous street gang" (Fleisher, 1995:152). Involvement of ex-convicts in youth gangs increases the life of the gangs and their level of violent crime, in part because of ex-convicts' increased proclivity to violence following imprisonment and the visibility and history they contribute to youth gangs (Moore, 1978).

Little treatment programming has been developed for gang members in juvenile detention and correctional facilities. Interpersonal skills training appears promising for improving social skills and reducing anger and, possibly, violence among street gang youth in institutionalized populations (Goldstein, 1993). The Aggression Replacement Training (ART) model teaches gang members anger control and other skills and has produced promising results with gangs in Brooklyn, NY, communities (Goldstein and Glick, 1994; Goldstein, Glick, and Gibbs, 1998). The model is being implemented in probation departments and detention centers in 28 counties throughout the State of Washington, in a number of juvenile institutions in the State of New York, and in the Texas Department of Youth (corrections). ART also has been used in community-based programs, such as the Mesa Gang Intervention Project, which is described on page 35.

A variety of gang awareness curriculums are used to help youth avoid gang involvement while they are incarcerated. One of these, Gang Awareness Necessary for Growth in Society, is used in California Youth Authority facilities (Duxbury, 1993). This curriculum has several elements: orientation; program overview; parole and the gang-active person; effects of gang violence; legal aspects of gang involvement; coping, responsibility, and accountability; and family, community, peer, cultural, and individual expectations.

Gang problems, correctional agencies' use of risk and needs assessments, and specialized programs to address gang problems in juvenile detention and correctional facilities are being assessed in an OJJDP-funded national survey conducted by the National Juvenile Detention Association. The initial report based on this survey (Howell et al., in press) covers gang problems and interventions in detention centers. Nearly 9 in 10 detention centers reported gang members among their residents. Almost half of the detention centers said that one-third or more of their inmates belonged to a gang. Slightly more than half of the detention centers reported gang-related assaults, almost half reported problems with gangs recruiting members, nearly one-third reported threats or intimidation of staff, and one-fourth reported threats or intimidation of nongang members.

Fifteen percent of the detention centers that were surveyed reported that they used no assessment procedures to identify gang members. Less than 2 percent performed a formal risk assessment, screened for classification, or used formal procedures for determination and management of security risk groups. Just 1 in 10 detention centers reported gearing certain programs toward gang members. Slightly more than 2 in 10 centers provided aftercare monitoring and support services for gang members. Aftercare is very important because of the high likelihood that these youth will return to active gang involvement in their communities, perhaps with their reputations enhanced by having served time in confinement.

Few of the programs geared toward gang members were deemed effective. On average, only 14 percent of respondents rated their programs "very effective" and less than half rated them "somewhat effective."

The most promising programs emphasized correction of educational deficiencies, vocational skills development (apprenticeships), drug abuse/use values and behavior change and treatment, and interpersonal and social skills development.

To deal more effectively with gang problems in facilities, juvenile detention and correctional facilities need to use risk assessments at intake, identify gang members, and properly classify offenders for security purposes. Better screening and risk classification of gang members would help protect staff and fellow inmates by giving correctional staff reliable information to classify gang members. Similarly, to achieve the best match between their treatment needs and available interventions, needs assessments should be made for all inmates. Finally, more program development is needed to prevent gang formation, help separate offenders from gangs, diminish the effectiveness of their recruitment efforts in detention centers, and prevent and reduce victimization of staff and fellow inmates. Progress in these areas should help break the cycle of gang members moving from detention centers and correctional facilities to prisons to communities.

In an earlier review of correctional programs for gang members, Duxbury (1993) made the following recommendations:

◆ Correctional policies and programs directed toward youth gangs and gang members should be coordinated with those of organizations engaged in prevention and suppression within a community or governmental jurisdiction.

◆ More systematic research should be conducted on correctional interventions with youth gang members.

◆ Individual correctional interventions should be based on objective classification of the gang members' risks and needs, including those related to gang participation.

◆ Institutional policies should create a climate in which youth feel sufficient safety to relinquish or refuse gang membership.

◆ Institutional programs should offer youth opportunities to develop their skills and knowledge so that, upon release, they will have the tools and self-esteem to choose activities other than illegal gang activities.

◆ Field supervision programs (parole/aftercare) should provide transitional services and, when appropriate, adequate surveillance to increase the likelihood that the released youth will make socially responsible choices.

One aftercare program for high-risk juveniles has been shown to produce very positive short-term effects (Josi and Sechrest, 1999). The Lifeskills '95 program, in San Bernardino and Riverside Counties, CA, serves youthful offenders released from the California Youth Authority. In addition to other impressive results, Lifeskills '95 reduced frequent gang contact. Only 8 percent of the Lifeskills '95 youth had frequent gang contact (versus 27 percent for the control group).

Suppression Programs

Intervention and suppression programs share the common goal of reducing criminal activities of gangs. Suppression programs use the full force of the law, generally through a combination of police, prosecution, and incarceration to deter the criminal activities of entire gangs, dissolve them, and remove individual gang members from them by means of prosecution and incarceration.

Following the use of gang suppression techniques in the Philadelphia CIN program, California criminal justice officials soon expanded the concept to prosecution and police programs (Klein, 1995a).

Prosecution Programs

Operation Hardcore, a prosecutorial gang suppression program, was created by the Los Angeles District Attorney's Office in 1979 and still operates under the office's Hardcore Gang Division (Genelin, 1993). It was the first prosecution program to target serious and violent juvenile gang-related offenses (Klein, Maxson, and Miller, 1995). Its distinctive features include vertical prosecution,[9] reduced

---

[9] The prosecutor who files a case remains responsible for it throughout the prosecution process.

caseloads, additional investigative support, and resources for assisting victims.

An independent evaluation of Operation Hardcore (Dahmann, 1981) showed that fewer dismissals; more convictions/adjudications, including more convictions/adjudications on the most serious charge; and a higher rate of State prison commitments/secure confinement dispositions were achieved for cases subject to the program than for cases undergoing the normal prosecutorial process. Dahmann concluded that "these results suggest that selective prosecution has been an effective strategy in Los Angeles and that the Operation Hardcore program has obtained demonstrable improvements in the criminal justice handling of gang defendants and their cases" (Dahmann, 1981:303). Operation Hardcore remains a highly regarded program.

Police Response

Police gang suppression programs for youth and adults (Klein, 1995a) drew impetus from the apparent growth of youth and adult gang problems in the Southwest in the early 1980's. Gang units were created in law enforcement departments to carry out gang intelligence, investigation, suppression, and prevention functions (Jackson and McBride, 1985; Klein, 1995a). Suppression tactics employed by the Los Angeles Police Department's (LAPD's) Community Resources Against Street Hoodlums (CRASH) operations, begun in the early 1980's, took the form of gang sweeps, hotspot targeting, and intensified patrols to apply pressure on gangs. Other terms used to characterize police suppression tactics include "saturation" of an area with police, "special surveillance" using modern technology, "zero tolerance," and "caravanning" (cruising neighborhoods in a caravan of patrol cars) (Klein, 1995a).

The most notorious gang sweep, Operation Hammer, was an LAPD CRASH operation launched in South Central Los Angeles in 1988 (Klein, 1995a). One thousand police officers swept through the area on a Friday night and again on Saturday, arresting likely gang members for a wide variety of offenses, including already-existing warrants, new traffic citations, curfew violations, gang-related behaviors, and observed criminal activities. All of those arrested (1,453 persons) were taken to a mobile booking

operation adjacent to Memorial Coliseum. Most of the arrested youth were released without charges. Slightly more than half were gang members. There were only 60 felony arrests, and charges were filed in only 32 instances. "This remarkably inefficient process was repeated many times, although with smaller forces—more typically one hundred or two hundred officers" (Klein, 1995a:162).

Recent police gang suppression strategies have been more innovative. In response to high levels of violence, the Baltimore City Police Department created a Violent Crimes Division that has several units, two of which are the Handgun Recovery Squad and the Youth Violence Strike Force. Violent gang members age 24 and under are targeted because analysis of internal police data on shootings reveals that more than half of victims and suspects are in this age category. Initially, the Handgun Recovery Squad seized guns from all over the city. "This proved ineffective, however, since seizing guns had no noticeable impact on crime" (Office of Juvenile Justice and Delinquency Prevention, 1999:98). Consequently, the squad limited its activities to targeting gangs in two hotspot areas, producing a marked decrease in handgun-related violence as evidenced by internal data collection. Handgun Recovery Squad efforts are buttressed by the Youth Violence Strike Force, which aggressively seeks to apprehend and incarcerate violent gang members by working closely with other Federal, State, and local agencies and in a team effort among police, parole, and probation officers. This initiative has not been evaluated.

St. Louis, MO, officials developed effective Consent to Search and Seize protocols in conjunction with its Firearm Suppression Program (FSP), which began in 1994 (Rosenfeld and Decker, 1996). Residential searches can be initiated by citizen requests for police service, reports from other police units, or by information gained from other investigations. Once the unit receives a report, two officers visit the residence in question, speak with an adult resident, and request permission to search the home for illegal weapons. Residents are informed that they will not be charged with the illegal possession of a firearm if they sign the Consent to Search and Seize form. In 1997, FSP was incorporated into a broader law enforcement initiative called Cease Fire (modeled after Boston's Operation Ceasefire) (Office of Juvenile

Justice and Delinquency Prevention, 1999). The St. Louis Cease Fire operation is coordinated across several law enforcement agencies and comprises three strategies:

◆ A crackdown on illicit gun trafficking through ATF's gun-tracing program.

◆ Swift response to acts of gang violence through intensive surveillance, youth outreach street-workers, and social service interventions.

◆ Operation Night Light (modeled after Boston's program, see page 30), which teams police with probation officers in visits to the homes of youth on probation to ensure compliance with the terms of their probation. (Probation officers have the authority to enter the homes of probationers unannounced while police must have search warrants.)

One Cease Fire component, the Gang Outreach program, was launched in 1998 by the St. Louis Police Department. This effort is part of St. Louis' attempt to implement the Comprehensive Community-Wide Approach to Gang Prevention, Intervention, and Suppression program through OJJDP's SafeFutures Program.[10] When a gang-involved youth is shot, counseling professionals discourage the victim from retaliating and encourage him or her to leave the gang. While the counselor is working with the victim, police make contact with the parent and, using the Consent to Search and Seize protocols, obtain permission to search the youth's home for weapons and other contraband. These new St. Louis components have not yet been evaluated.

The Los Angeles Police Department's Operation Cul de Sac (OCDS), launched in 1990, erected traffic barriers in neighborhoods in which gangs and accompanying gang crime "had spiraled out of control" (Lasley, 1998:1). OCDS was an experiment to determine whether traffic barriers could be used effectively to "design out" crime by reducing the opportunities to commit crime. The assumption underlying the experi-

ment was that gang violence, including homicide, is partly the result of criminal opportunity. OCDS postulated that violent gang crime could be deterred because the opportunities—in this case, major roadways that facilitate entrance to and exit from high-crime neighborhoods—could be controlled. Thus, traffic barriers were used to decrease the mobility of rival gangs traveling to and from gang crime hotspots in a 10-block area. Police closed all major roads leading to and from the identified hotspots by placing freeway dividers at the end of the streets that led directly to the hotspots. This reconfiguration essentially created cul-de-sacs, which could hamper "hit-and-run" crimes such as drive-by shootings.

Lasley (1998) compared crime levels in the OCDS area before, during, and after its 2 years of operation with crime levels in a site in which OCDS did not operate. The study found that gang-related homicides and assaults in the OCDS area fell significantly during program operation and rose in the year after program cessation. Crime levels remained constant in the comparison area. It did not appear that OCDS displaced gang crime to contiguous neighborhoods. The program did not seem to have any effect on property crimes. Because this program was conducted in only one site, Lasley cautioned that these results could not be guaranteed in other communities and that further evaluations were needed to confirm the effectiveness of traffic barriers in reducing serious gang crime. A longer evaluation period is advisable because studies show that peaks and valleys in violent gang-related crimes occur at different times in different communities (Block and Block, 1993; Decker, 1996; Howell, 1999; Howell and Decker, 1999; Klein, 1995b).

Several researchers have noted that youth and adult gang problems have not decreased appreciably for a significant period of time in areas where only suppression programs have been implemented (Klein, 1995a; Moore, 1978, 1991; Spergel, 1995) and that the effectiveness of police crackdowns generally has been short-lived (Sherman, 1990).

One of the most respected law enforcement gang suppression programs for youth and adults, the Los Angeles County Sheriff Department's Operation Safe Streets (OSS), began in 1979 with the assignment of teams of gang investigators to four sheriff's

---

[10] For more information on the Comprehensive Community-Wide Approach, see pages 34–37. The SafeFutures Program assists six different communities, St. Louis among them, with "existing collaboration efforts to reduce youth violence and delinquency . . . [and] also seeks to improve the service delivery system by creating a continuum of care responsive to the needs of youth and their families" (Kracke, 1996).

station areas that were combating a tremendous amount of youth and adult gang violence (McBride, 1993). Each team identified and investigated the most active gang in its geographical area, concentrating law enforcement resources exclusively on the targeted gang and its members. These suppression activities were combined with vertical prosecution and intensive probation supervision. McBride (1993) suggested that, apart from the combination of these three elements, a key to the success of the program was the personal rapport investigators established with gang members by maintaining regular contact with them. This helped penetrate the cloak of personal anonymity, which typically helps gang members terrorize communities. At the same time, this rapport led investigators to begin seeking educational, job placement, and family counseling programs for the youth gang members. As McBride (1993:413) observed, "The investigators found that, as they applied firm but fair law enforcement and used their personal knowledge of the gang members, backed by a demonstrated humanitarian concern for the status of the individual, violence within the targeted gangs began to decline." Jackson and McBride (1985) referred to this approach as "working" gangs using traditional investigation techniques. Soon, communities in the targeted areas began to respond positively to OSS operations. McBride (1993) reported a 50-percent decrease in youth and adult gang activity.

Five gang-related programs supported by the Office of Community Oriented Policing Services (COPS) have shown promising results: the Antigang Initiative in Dallas, TX, and the Youth Firearms Violence Initiatives (YFVI's) in Inglewood, CA; Milwaukee, WI; Salinas, CA; and Seattle, WA. Because the last four of these programs targeted youth gun use, they have the potential to reduce gang homicide.

Antigang Initiative, Dallas, TX. In 1996 and 1997, this COPS initiative targeted five geographical areas that were home to seven of the city's most violent gangs. Three main suppression strategies were employed:

◆ Saturation patrols/high-visibility patrols in target areas. These patrols stopped and frisked suspected gang members and made appropriate arrests.

◆ Aggressive curfew enforcement. Ordinances were strictly enforced whenever suspected gang members were encountered.

◆ Aggressive enforcement of truancy laws and regulations. Police worked in conjunction with school districts to curb truancy.

Gang unit officers teamed with community policing officers to carry out selected strategies in each of the five geographical areas.

By examining weekly and monthly police reports that documented overtime-funded activities, evaluators determined which of the three suppression strategies various Dallas police teams mainly used (Fritsch, Caeti, and Taylor, 1999). Patrol beats that had a similar number of gang-related violent offenses in a 1-year period prior to the antigang initiative were selected for comparative evaluation purposes. Gang-related violent offenses reported to the police before and during the initiative were analyzed in both target and control areas. The analysis showed that gang-related violence decreased significantly during 1996–97 in both target and control areas; however, the decrease was more substantial in targeted areas (57 percent versus 37 percent). The larger decrease in gang-related violence in targeted areas was attributed to the use of two combined strategies: aggressive enforcement of curfew, and truancy laws and regulations. Traditional (undirected) saturation patrol did not produce significant reductions when used as the main suppression strategy. The authors advise that these "results must be interpreted with caution and replicated across and within several jurisdictions before broad and definitive conclusions can be drawn about the usefulness of a particular strategy" (Fritsch, Caeti, and Taylor, 1999:129–130).

Youth Firearms Violence Initiative, Inglewood, CA. This COPS initiative sought to reduce handgun violence through the disruption of the activities of two gangs—the Crenshaw Mafia Gang and the Family Gangster Bloods—in a public housing area of West Central Los Angeles, known as "the Bottoms" (Office of Juvenile Justice and Delinquency Prevention, 1999). A mentoring program, Rights of Passage, was implemented to fill the gap in afterschool activities from 3 to 6 p.m. Strategies Against Gang

Environments (SAGE), which comprised police officers, a deputy district attorney, and a deputy probation officer, conducted saturation patrols in the target area. Buttressed by an antiloitering civil injunction against the Crenshaw Mafia Gang, SAGE officers were able to implement a proactive approach rather than wait for a crime to occur. Although the SAGE unit disbanded after YFVI funding was exhausted, the injunction against the Crenshaw Mafia Gang remains in place and is enforced through routine patrols and the police department's gang component. The police department reports that the Crenshaw Mafia Gang "has ceased to exist as an organized entity as a direct result of the civil action" and effective police enforcement (Office of Juvenile Justice and Delinquency Prevention, 1999).

Youth Firearms Violence Initiative, Milwaukee, WI. This COPS initiative sought to deter gun carrying in high-crime hotspots (Office of Juvenile Justice and Delinquency Prevention, 1999). Suppression components included strengthening the police department's gang crimes/intelligence unit, enhancing curfew activities, and deploying saturation patrols in high crime areas. Target areas were determined by geographic information system data that indicated a high incidence of juvenile handgun violence. Decreases in firearm-related offenses, including violent firearm offenses, have been attributed to the YFVI initiative (Office of Juvenile Justice and Delinquency Prevention, 1999).

Youth Firearms Violence Initiative, Salinas, CA. This COPS initiative targets gang members under age 25 (Office of Juvenile Justice and Delinquency Prevention, 1999). Its primary component is a violence suppression unit, a team of 15 police officers who use aggressive patrol strategies, including periodic surveillance, probation/patrol services, traffic stops, raids, and search warrants to recover illegal firearms used in crimes. YFVI operations are supported by a database that geographically tracks gang-related activity and firearm use. This database allows police officers to respond to inquiries regarding the location of firearm seizures, violent crimes, and gang incidents near school zones. Decreases in gun-related and violent crimes and gang presence have been attributed to YFVI operations (Office of Juvenile Justice and Delinquency Prevention, 1999).

Youth Firearms Violence Initiative, Seattle, WA. The overall goal of this COPS initiative was to reduce youth firearm violence through targeted and focused enforcement efforts (Office of Juvenile Justice and Delinquency Prevention, 1999). This YFVI comprised several components: the Seattle Team for Youth, which is still in existence, provides intensive services for youth who were in gangs or were otherwise at risk of gang involvement; deployment of school-emphasis patrol officers to work in various prevention, intervention, and school safety projects; and school enforcement teams of officers who worked closely with school administrators to reduce youth firearm violence. A key component of the Seattle YFVI was the creation of a system for tracking the city's 50 most violent juveniles, many of whom were affiliated with gangs. Police and probation officers were paired to increase surveillance of these juveniles and to enforce probation conditions. In addition, enhanced prosecution was instituted. An overall increase in arrests for weapons violations and a decline in weapons violations in the Seattle schools during the life of the program have been reported (Office of Juvenile Justice and Delinquency Prevention, 1999).

Weisel and Painter (1997) have provided detailed case studies of police responses to youth and adult gang problems in Austin, TX; Chicago, IL; Kansas City, MO; Metro Dade County, FL; and San Diego, CA. These sites were selected for the severity of their youth and adult gang and drug problems, for regional diversity, for ethnic variation in gang problems, and for variations in their approaches to local gang problems. These case studies are unique in their long-term perspective, providing a view of how each police department's approach changed over a 5-year period, from 1991–92 to 1996. Three issues guided the studies: events that stimulated each police department to respond to existing youth and adult gang problems, key aspects of each police department's strategic response, and outcomes in each jurisdiction.

Several conclusions can be drawn from the Weisel and Painter case studies with respect to youth and adult gangs:

◆ Ethnic variation in gang membership was a distinguishing characteristic in all of the studied sites. Although a particular ethnic group predominated in most gangs, the observed trend was toward racially mixed gangs.

◆ The types of criminal activity varied widely from gang to gang and from one site to another. According to the authors, "In some places, gang activity, drug activity and weapons violations are nearly synonymous terms; in other areas of the same city, the nexus may be much looser, with drug activity peripheral to other criminal activity. In other areas, drug usage is merely a recreational activity of gang members" (Weisel and Painter, 1997:77).

◆ Police in the five sites consistently reported gangs to be less structured and organized than they had previously believed. Those Chicago gangs that are highly structured and extensively involved in drug trafficking are the exception, not the rule.

◆ Police responses varied as much as the nature of gang problems. Their responses also changed: from an approach emphasizing suppression, intelligence gathering, and investigation in 1991 to a more comprehensive approach in 1996 that integrated investigations, intelligence gathering, prevention, community policing, and enforcement activities in a collaborative effort with community organizations.

◆ With notable exceptions, most patrol officers had received no training in how to identify gang activity. Consequently, their reports yielded inconsistent and unreliable data. Differences in reporting guidelines and disparity in gang definitions also produced wide variations in the quality of reporting on gang incidents.

◆ The police departments studied lacked uniform methods for determining the effectiveness of their antigang efforts. Despite the absence of evidence regarding effectiveness, however, "it appears that specific strategies used by police agencies work best when targeted at specific behaviors, locations, and individuals" (Weisel and Painter, 1997:89).

Geomapping and Tracking Systems

Recent technological advances in police tracking and management of gang crime include computer map-

ping, object-oriented databases, management information systems, and offender identification and tracking (Fritsch, Caeti, and Taylor, 1999). The mayor of Houston, TX, instituted an Anti-Gang Office and Task Force in the early 1990's that developed a computerized gang geomapping and tracking system to identify the location of gangs and gang-related gun violence and the location of existing youth program resources (Office of Juvenile Justice and Delinquency Prevention, 1999). Hotspots of gang activity and necessary youth services are linked through this information system. The Gang Education Awareness Resistance program, a partnership between the Anti-Gang Office, the school district, and two police departments, helps schools with gang-related security problems. The Gang Prevention Program of the Association for the Advancement of Mexican Americans provides legal education and a wide range of services for at-risk youth. A regional gang-related information tracking system is serving more than 50 Houston-area law enforcement agencies. Although it has not been evaluated, the Anti-Gang Office and Task Force is a promising city-level management initiative.

The Chicago, IL, Police Department has constructed one of the most accessible and easy-to-use tracking programs in the Nation. Called the Information Collection for Automated Mapping (ICAM) program, it uses computerized mapping to help police track criminal activity in neighborhoods. Combined with geocoding (which verifies addresses and links to other geographic information), computer mapping software can combine data sets to provide a multidimensional view of gang crime and its potential contributing factors (see Block and Block, 1993, for illustrations of the kind of information that can be compiled with this system).

The Orange County, CA, Gang Incident Tracking System (GITS) is another type of gang information system that supports not only intelligence and gang crime reporting functions, but also evaluation of community interventions (Vila and Meeker, 1997). Twenty-two independent cities and the Orange County Sheriff-Coroner's Department report to a centralized database. Geographical information software is used to analyze the GITS data, generating geomaps of gang crimes and the residency of gang members. An analysis of more than 7,500 arrests

Identification of Gang Members

Determining a particular individual's gang involvement is as difficult as identifying true youth gangs. In many instances, a youth may associate occasionally with a gang, participate episodically in the activities of a gang, or desire gang membership without actually being a member. Likewise, many youth leave gangs by drifting out, gradually dissociating themselves. Because severe criminal sanctions can be applied to gang membership in certain jurisdictions, a valid determination is important. The National Drug Intelligence Center (1995) recommended that investigators use these criteria (any one of which qualifies the individual) for determining whether a youth is a gang member:

◆ The individual admits membership in a gang (i.e., self-reported).

◆ A law enforcement agency or reliable informant identifies an individual as a gang member.

◆ An informant of previously untested reliability identifies an individual as a gang member, and this information is corroborated by an independent source.

◆ The individual resides in or frequents a particular gang's area and adopts its style of dress, use of hand signs, symbols, or tattoos; maintains ongoing relationships with known gang members; and has been arrested several times in the company of identified gang members for offenses consistent with usual gang activity.

◆ There is reasonable suspicion that the individual is involved in a gang-related criminal activity or enterprise.

Determining gang membership of youth brought into the juvenile justice system may be more problematic because of a lack of information in their official records. In a national assessment, Spergel and Curry (1993) surveyed juvenile justice and social service agencies to identify the criteria used to distinguish between gang and nongang members. Agencies used nine different methods that fell into two categories (the percentage of respondents using each criterion is indicated in parentheses):

Direct Observation or Agency Information

◆ Symbols/symbolic behavior (51 percent).

◆ Self-admission (47 percent).

◆ Association with gang members (39 percent).

◆ Type of criminal behavior (34 percent).

◆ Location or residence (14 percent).

Reports of Membership From Other Agencies or Individuals

◆ Police identification (42 percent).

◆ Informant identification (40 percent).

◆ Other legal identification (19 percent).

◆ Other institutional identification (16 percent).

from 1995 to 1998 showed that adults were involved in 46 percent more violent arrests than juveniles and that a much larger proportion of adult arrests were for a violent crime (Wiebe, Meeker, and Vila, in press). The researchers concluded that adult gangs in Orange County committed more serious crime than juvenile gangs.

Recently, gang suppression tactics have been expanded in three directions: (1) collaborative approaches that tie together all sectors of the community; (2) State laws that increase criminal sanctions for gang crime and gang involvement, and local ordinances and enforcement of specific criminal codes that restrict gang activities; and (3) multiagency and multijurisdictional approaches that bring together several law enforcement agencies. These strategies are discussed in the sections that follow.

Strategies Using Multiple Techniques

A number of communities have developed gang strategies that integrate two or more techniques. Such communities typically are guided by a local task force formed to curb gang involvement and violence. Community policing also is often used with other techniques.

Community Policing

Community policing programs appear to have realized some success in dealing with youth gang problems. Cronin (1994) describes the Norfolk Police Assisted Community Enforcement program, which has a gang component and is focused in low-income housing areas. A second community policing model that targets youth gangs is a Reno, NV, program (Weston, 1995). Through the formation of a Community Action Team (CAT), the Reno Police Department involves representatives from minority neighborhoods, officials from community service agencies, and political leaders in a community solution to the city's serious youth gang problem (Weston, 1995). The CAT program has two strategies: (1) creation of a highly specialized team of officers to target the top 5 percent of violent gang members in a repeat offender program and (2) a prevention and early intervention program that targets an estimated 80 percent of Reno's gang members who are not considered to be hardcore. Neighborhood advisory groups provide feedback from community residents, and an interagency group coordinates prevention and intervention resources. Although the program has not been independently evaluated, local officials are convinced it is effective and continue to support its operations (Weston, 1995). A third community policing model, in the Redlands, CA, Police Department, incorporates a new scientific approach: "risk-focused policing" (Rich, 1999). The model is based on the extensive research literature on risk and protective factors. Data related to these factors, adolescent problem behaviors, and existing programs are entered into a database. Mapping software displays the results by census block. To prevent delinquency and gang involvement more effectively, the police department focuses its resources on areas that most need risk reduction and protection enhancement.

Community-University Model for Gang Intervention and Delinquency Prevention in Small Cities

Takata and Tyler (1994) assisted Racine, WI (population, 84,298), in developing the Community-University Model for Gang Intervention and Delinquency Prevention in Small Cities, which also can be adapted for larger cities. This team model consists of six major steps that communities experiencing an emerging gang problem can take:

◆ **A genuine commitment to youth.** This can be demonstrated by working directly with youth, developing an understanding of their problems and concerns, building trust, and empowering them to solve problems. The team must demonstrate a commitment to resolving local issues (e.g., the need for recreational facilities in minority neighborhoods) and develop a thorough understanding of the city's social, political, and economic context, especially race and ethnic relations.

◆ **Gang problem assessment.** The team will need to investigate, observe, and document the developing gang problem while learning from neighboring jurisdictions through the exchange of information. The team must understand the basis for initial denial of gang problems by some groups, agencies, and individuals. Meetings with community leaders and individuals must be organized. In all likelihood, a catalyzing event will occur, if it has not already, that forces recognition of the problem.

◆ **Initial networking.** A task force should be formed to collaborate on possible solutions. Its work includes organizing community meetings and neighborhood hearings to identify solutions and develop a collaborative response to gangs.

◆ **Local study of the gang situation.** The task force should identify a local college, university, or other community resource that can study the local gang problem. This study would provide the documentation necessary to secure external funding for the programs the task force identifies. Initial funding might be sought to implement one or two of the task force's recommendations (e.g., community collaboration). The task force should be alert to politicization of its work by opposition parties.

◆ **Timeout.** In this stage, the task force should publish and disseminate research findings, expand its network via conferences and other communication outlets, identify funding sources, establish political foundations for funding, and prepare grant/contract applications for the second set of awards.

◆ **Development of new programs.** The final stage is program development and implementation. The overall plan should include long-term goals and a master plan. New programs should be implemented through continued collaborative efforts. Research and program development would continue during the implementation of the program.

Other communities have organized their gang assessment, planning, and program development initiatives in similar steps.

Aurora Gang Task Force

Aurora, CO, formed the all-volunteer Aurora Gang Task Force (AGTF) in 1989 (Atkinson, 1996). The members of AGTF come from volunteer organizations, churches, social services, government agencies, the military, the media, and businesses. AGTF promotes programs for at-risk youth, lobbies for legislation to better control youth and adult gang-related behavior, advocates tougher prosecution and sentencing for youth and adult gang-related crime, and disseminates information about youth and adult gangs to the media, other interested agencies, the public, and community groups. AGTF also supports other city initiatives. One of these, the High Intensity Community Oriented Policing program, uses gang sweeps to control youth and adult gang-related drug trafficking and police area representatives assigned to assist citizens in keeping gang crime out of their neighborhoods.

Aurora was honored by the National Conference of Mayors' 1992 City Livability Awards program for its efforts to mobilize an effective response to youth and adult gangs. Gang-related statistics compiled by the Aurora Police Department show mixed results. Although youth and adult gang arrests dropped, drug trafficking involving gangs increased, and "a conclusive solution to the gang problem remained frustratingly elusive" (Atkinson, 1996:261). Nevertheless, AGTF is considered a broad-based model for dealing with youth and adult gangs (Bureau of

Justice Assistance, 1997b), with community policing serving as a key component.

Partnership for a Safer Cleveland

Cleveland's Task Force on Violent Crime (now called the Partnership for a Safer Cleveland) was formed in 1981 and enjoyed early success in dealing with gangs (Trump, 1996; Walker and Schmidt, 1996). Until 1989, however, city officials denied that the city had a gang problem. They then began to respond to Huff's (1989) research on Cleveland youth and adult gangs. The task force recommended that the Cleveland Police Department form a youth gang unit. Numerous other recommendations for the creation and expansion of programs and collaborative efforts were made and acted upon, and some of this work is still ongoing. A key feature of the task force's approach was its scope: the city's gang problem was assessed and responded to in the context of broader juvenile crime and drug problems.

The task force and the police department's youth gang unit concentrated part of their efforts on decreasing the presence of gangs in Cleveland's schools. This work paid off (Trump, 1996). School gang incidents decreased 39 percent citywide in just 2 years through the following integrated activities: prioritized enforcement, investigation, and intervention in school gang-related incidents citywide; staff, parent, and student antigang education; a truancy program; and a variety of coordinated programs designed to reduce gang activity and provide alternatives to gang involvement.

SARA

Another model for engaging communities in a gang problem-solving process, called SARA for each of its sequential steps—scanning, analysis, response, and assessment—is used by the Bureau of Justice Assistance (1997a) in the development of citywide and multijurisdictional enforcement strategies to investigate and prosecute drug distribution and related crimes committed by urban (mainly adult) street gangs. SARA is based on the principles of problem-oriented policing—proactively identifying problems, understanding the underlying causes of those problems, and developing interventions to address them (Goldstein, 1979, 1990).

Multiagency Initiatives

Many cities and counties claim success in pooling resources with Federal and State agencies to combat youth and adult gangs and related violence.[11] Multiagency initiatives generally are of two types. The most common type is Federal, State, and local law enforcement collaboration across jurisdictional boundaries. In other instances, crime control agencies (e.g., police, prosecutors, courts) collaborate in targeting gangs.

Los Angeles Metropolitan Task Force

California has become a leader in designing and implementing multiagency initiatives that draw on both Federal and local resources (National Criminal Justice Association, 1997). One of the most successful antigang initiatives, the Los Angeles Metropolitan Task Force, grew out of the city's 1992 riots, in which youth and adult gangs were blamed for much of the damage. Its original mission was to identify and prosecute individuals responsible for the riots (U.S. General Accounting Office, 1996). Led by the FBI, in collaboration with local police, the Los Angeles task force was assisted by ATF. This assistance included the use of Federal laws and authority (e.g., with prosecution, wiretapping, and witness security); money to purchase firearms undercover and pay informants; and logistical support. More than 2,000 arrests were made between February 1992 and September 1995, of which nearly 1,000 were for violent crimes (U.S. General Accounting Office, 1996). Nearly 300 Federal and State convictions resulted from these arrests, more than three-fourths of which were for violent crime charges.

Some Federal and local officials interviewed by U.S. General Accounting Office staff in 1995 and 1996 credited the Los Angeles task force with reducing crime rates in some neighborhoods and making it safe for children to play outside again. As a general assessment, most line officers mentioned "long-term, proactive investigations of entire gangs as an advantageous element differentiating the federal task force approach to violent crime from the local law enforcement approach, which generally involves short-term, reactive investigations of individual gang members" (U.S. General Accounting Office, 1996:3). The U.S. Department of Justice (1996) has noted the success of the task force.

Boston Gun Project

The Boston Gun Project is a suppression program that targets youth and adult gang members in a multiagency effort (Clark, 1997).[12] It is based on an analysis of homicide among Boston's youth (age 21 and under) that determined that this violence is gang centered, neighborhood based, and concentrated in a small number of repeat-offending, gang-involved youth. The program was initiated in individual neighborhoods with an explicit communication campaign. This campaign begins with an orientation for community groups and is then often carried out face-to-face with gang members, who are given the message that gang violence has provoked a zero tolerance approach and that only an end to gang violence will stop new gang-focused suppression activities. The long sentences that offenders receive are publicized in high-crime neighborhoods. The program components described above build upon and integrate the efforts of grassroots organizations and the faith community.

A multiagency, coordinated task force of 45 full-time Boston police officers and others from outside agencies suppresses youth and adult gang violence and gun use (Kennedy, Piehl, and Braga, 1996). Suppression tactics include "pulling levers" to impose costs on offenders related to their chronic offending by serving warrants, enforcing probation restrictions, and deploying Federal enforcement powers (Kennedy, 1997).

Under another component of the program—Operation Night Light—police and probation officers, working in teams, make nightly visits to the homes of youth on probation to ensure that they are complying with the terms and conditions of their probation. This helps

---

[11] Many of the programs and strategies reviewed in the remainder of this Summary are used to target adult criminal organizations, which sometimes are called "gangs," and purely drug-trafficking gangs, which are not normally considered youth gangs (Klein, 1995a). Unfortunately, research and practice to date do not permit distinguishing which interventions are most likely to work best with youth gangs versus other (mainly adult) criminal groups that are also called gangs.

[12] Gangs were defined here as a "self-identified group of kids who act corporately (at least sometimes) and violently (at least sometimes)" (Kennedy, Piehl, and Braga, 1996:158).

target tough enforcement efforts against gang leaders. City "streetworkers" (gang prevention and mediation specialists) also work in tandem with police and probation officers, helping resolve conflicts and linking youth who want help with needed services.

Simultaneously, the Boston Gun Project seeks to interrupt the self-sustaining cycle of fear, weapon use, and violence that appears to be driving youth violence in the city by reducing use of guns with a "coerced use-reduction" strategy and reducing access to firearms (Kennedy, Piehl, and Braga, 1996). To carry out this deterrence strategy, gang mediation specialists are deployed to gang hotspots, which are generally already known through mapping that shows gang overlap, intergang conflicts, and gun-related crime. Heightened surveillance for shootings, assaults, and other selected incidents triggers deployment of interagency crisis intervention teams with "swift and comprehensive attention." After this "calming" operation, patrol officers continue to monitor the hotspot for reoccurrence of gun violence.

The strategy that reduces access to firearms, using gun-tracing capabilities of the Boston Police Department and ATF, seeks to disrupt the illicit gun market. The rationale supporting the supply-reduction strategy is that disruption of the illicit market will interrupt fear-driven gun acquisition and use, thereby reducing gang violence in Boston. Using Federal firearm laws, the project "makes the market much less hospitable by strategically removing the most dangerous gang and drug offenders from the streets, and stemming the flow of firearms into Massachusetts" (Kennedy, Piehl, and Braga, 1996:5).

Evaluation results are not yet available, although gun homicide victimization among 14- to 24-year-olds in Boston is reported to have fallen by two-thirds since the project began (Kennedy, 1997). Because homicides were dropping nationwide among this age group during the project period, the evaluation will compare Boston's homicide trends to trends in a sample of other cities (Kennedy, 1997).

Bureau of Justice Assistance Gang Suppression Prototype

The Bureau of Justice Assistance (BJA) (1997a, 1997b) has developed a suppression prototype for drug-trafficking youth and adult gangs that focuses almost exclusively on law enforcement and prosecution strategies (see also Kelling et al., 1998, for information on BJA's comprehensive community programs that target youth and adult gangs). It is modeled after BJA's Urban Street Gang Program and is composed of projects in seven demonstration sites, some of which are administered by police departments, others by prosecutors' offices. The prototype consists of six key program elements: planning and analysis, gang information and intelligence systems, gang suppression strategies and tactics, interagency cooperation and collaboration, use of legal mechanisms, and evaluation of operations. The BJA Report *Urban Street Gang Involvement* provides detailed information on each of these elements. Gang suppression strategies and tactics in the BJA prototype include:[13]

◆ Confidential informants and undercover officers.

◆ Surveillance/arrest, buy/bust, and reverse sting operations.

◆ Interdiction, barriers, sweeps, and warrant execution.

◆ Other investigative approaches, such as surveillance, followup investigations, and multijurisdictional task forces.

◆ Suppression through patrol, including directed patrol and community oriented policing.

◆ Suppression through enforcement of health, building, and zoning codes and nuisance abatement ordinances.

Descriptions of two examples of multiagency strategies that are consistent with the BJA prototype follow.

A small multiagency task force successfully dismantled New York City's Puerto Rican Black Park Gang,

---

[13] See Bureau of Justice Assistance (1997b:62–72) for detailed descriptions of these suppression tactics.

so named because it shot out lights surrounding its base of operations in a park to avoid police detection (Bureau of Justice Assistance, 1997b). It was a very violent drug gang—believed to be responsible for 15 murders—that trafficked in drugs and used the proceeds to buy legitimate businesses through which it laundered drug profits. The investigation was led by the homicide investigation unit of the New York County (Manhattan) District Attorney's Office and joined by the New York City Police Department, other New York agencies, and several Federal agencies, including the FBI, the Drug Enforcement Administration, and ATF.

Tactics used included intensive study and initial surveillance, infiltration of the gang by undercover officers, cultivation and use of confidential informants, electronic surveillance, cooperation with probation and parole officers, and asset forfeiture. The success of the effort resulted in initiating recreation programs in the park sponsored by the Police Athletic League and renaming it White Light Park because lighting had been restored (Bureau of Justice Assistance, 1997b).

The Jurisdictions United for Drug Gang Enforcement (JUDGE) program in San Diego coordinates investigations, prosecutions, and the sanctioning of criminal youth and adult gang members (Bureau of Justice Assistance, 1997b). This suppression program, headed by the district attorney's gang unit, targets violent members of drug-trafficking gangs. Several elements are deemed critical to its success: a motivated and reliable informant; a vertical prosecution team that works with investigators from the operation's beginning; a principal prosecutor freed from responsibility for other cases; videotape corroboration of drug transactions using paid informants; coordination with judges; and coordination with the jail before a sweep to allow preparation for the increased number of detainees. Still in operation, JUDGE also enforces conditions of probation and drug laws and provides vertical prosecution for probation violations and new offenses involving targeted offenders. The JUDGE strategy has been replicated in Oceanside, CA, and in Seattle, WA.

Minnesota Statewide Task Force

Minnesota created a statewide gang task force, composed of 40 members from local, county, and State police agencies, enabling law enforcement to collaborate effectively across jurisdictions (Office of Juvenile Justice and Delinquency Prevention, 1999). Members are deputized, have statewide power, and conduct long-term investigations using a gang database. This task force grew out of Minnesota HEALS (Hope, Education, and Law and Safety), a public-private partnership initiated by Honeywell, Inc., that has more than 60 members, including several other corporations, State and local law enforcement agencies, and a wide variety of other representatives. Gang suppression activities are concentrated in the Minneapolis Anti-Violence Initiative, which employs police-probation teams modeled after Boston's Operation Night Light program (described on page 30; see also Corbet, 1998; Corbet, Fitzgerald, and Jordan, 1996). These teams target gang members who possess weapons and are multiple offenders. Suppression strategies include saturation patrols, rapid response teams to prevent retaliation, gun tracing, Federal prosecution in cases involving guns, and vertical prosecution. Decreases in gang-related serious and violent crimes have been attributed to the Minneapolis HEALS partnership (Office of Juvenile Justice and Delinquency Prevention, 1999).

Federal Initiatives

Violent and drug-trafficking gangs are targeted in the Clinton Administration's Anti-Violent Crime Initiative through the use of Federal, State, and local interjurisdictional task forces (Office of the Attorney General, 1995; U.S. General Accounting Office, 1996). The Attorney General (1995) reported that the Drug Enforcement Administration uses Mobile Enforcement Teams (MET's) that work with State and local law enforcement authorities to dismantle drug organizations. The Houston, TX, MET was deployed in Galveston, where a high rate of juvenile homicides was attributed to drug-trafficking problems caused by three street gangs. MET made 17 arrests of gang members, 13 of whom were charged with violent crimes.

TARGET

The Tri-Agency Resource Gang Enforcement Team (TARGET) integrates and coordinates the work of the Orange County, CA, police and sheriff's departments, the Orange County District Attorney, and the Orange County Probation Department (Capizzi, Cook, and Schumacher, 1995). Its aim is to reduce gang crime by selectively incarcerating the most violent and repeat gang offenders (based on their criminal records) in the most violent gangs in Orange County. Once identified, these offenders are monitored closely for new offenses and undergo intensive supervision when on probation for violation of probation terms and conditions. TARGET ensures close collaboration among law enforcement staff, probation officers, and prosecutors by housing TARGET teams in police and sheriff's departments. Each team consists of police officers who serve as gang investigators, a probation officer, a deputy district attorney, and a district attorney investigator. The TARGET process "involves quickly identifying the leaders of gangs, concentrating on them (targeting) for enforcement efforts, conducting searches, and making arrests" (Rackauckas, 1999:9). Police gang investigators are well trained to deal with hostile witnesses, and deputy district attorneys and district attorney investigators are experienced in the vertical prosecution of cases through the court system, which appears to be a key element in program success. Begun in Westminster in 1992, TARGET has been replicated in six additional areas within Orange County. Currently, 12 TARGET teams are operating in 8 cities in the county and in the South Orange Sheriff's Department.

The effectiveness of the TARGET teams is impressive. During its first 2 years of operation, TARGET teams identified and verified 647 individual gang members, 77 of whom were targeted as high-rate offenders and gang leaders. Two-thirds of them were placed in custody while awaiting trial, and a 99-percent conviction rate was achieved along with a 62-percent decrease in serious gang-related crime (Kent and Smith, 1995). This level of success has continued with TARGET's subsequent expansion. In 1998, there were 3,475 filings of criminal charges against gang members, which included more than 2,600 Street Terrorism Enforcement and Prevention (STEP) Act charges and/or enhancements

(Rackauckas, 1999). All types of criminal incidents—except for drug-related offenses, which do not constitute a major gang activity in Orange County—have dropped steadily since 1994, including a 57-percent drop in gang homicides since 1993 (Rackauckas, 1999). An evaluation of the program showed a sharp increase in incarceration of gang members (in juvenile detention and correctional facilities, jails, the California Youth Authority, and State prisons) and a cumulative 47-percent decrease in gang crime over a 7-year period (Kent et al., 2000). In one case, the Costa Mesa TARGET team dismantled a gang by convicting and incarcerating the gang's leaders and placing on restrictive probation gang members not sent to prison (Orange County Chiefs' and Sheriff's Association, 1999). In another initiative, the Santa Ana TARGET team—the Street Terrorism Offender Project (STOP)—set out to reduce violence between two rival gangs and other gang crime in the hotspot area in which they operated. An evaluation using Gang Incident Tracking System (a database of gang crime incidents and arrests in Orange County) data showed that after an initial increase in arrest incidents involving the two gangs (as a direct result of STOP actions), crimes involving the two gangs and the overall level of gang crime in the targeted hotspot decreased significantly over the next 2 years to near zero (Wiebe, 1998).

Klein and colleagues (1995:292) suggested that "focused efforts of this type can produce positive effects in smaller gang cities." TARGET won the National League of Cities 1993 award for Exemplary Local Government Criminal Justice Programs.

Comprehensive Approaches to Gang Problems

Klein (1995a:153) makes the case that communities need to organize themselves to deal with youth gangs:

> Street gangs are by-products of partially incapacitated communities. Until we dedicate the state and federal resources necessary to alter these community structures, gangs will continue to emerge despite value transformation, suppression, or other community efforts. I'm talking about the most obvious resources—jobs, better schools, social services, health programs, family

support, training in community organization skills, and support for resident empowerment. That's easy to say but obviously not easy to do.

A more comprehensive approach, combining program elements such as social services, crisis intervention, gang suppression, and community involvement, might be more effective than a one-dimensional approach. For evaluation results that suggest this, see Spergel and Grossman (1997) and Spergel, Grossman, and Wa (1998). Three community-based and coordinated approaches designed to deal comprehensively with the youth gang problem are detailed here.

The Comprehensive Community-Wide Approach to Gang Prevention, Intervention, and Suppression

OJJDP's Comprehensive Community-Wide Approach to Gang Prevention, Intervention, and Suppression program is designed to implement and test a comprehensive model for reducing youth gang violence. In 1999, after funding the demonstration and testing sites for 4 years, OJJDP decided to continue supporting two of the five sites based on their strong prospects for sustaining the approach, program performance, preliminary evaluation data, and evidence of the development of promising strategies. Although Bloomington, IL; Tucson, AZ; and San Antonio, TX, served as promising demonstration sites, Riverside, CA, and Mesa, AZ, were chosen to receive the additional support. The program utilizes the OJJDP Comprehensive Gang Model, or the Spergel model, as it is often called, to engage communities in a systematic gang assessment, consensus building, and program development process. The model involves delivering the following five core strategies through an integrated and team-oriented problem-solving approach:[14]

◆ **Community mobilization,** including citizens, youth, community groups, and agencies.

◆ **Provision of academic, economic, and social opportunities.** Special school training and job programs are especially critical for older gang members who are not in school but may be ready to leave the gang or decrease participation in criminal gang activity for many reasons, including maturation and the need to provide for family.

◆ **Social intervention,** using street outreach workers to engage gang-involved youth.

◆ **Gang suppression,** including formal and informal social control procedures of the juvenile and criminal justice systems and community agencies and groups. Community-based agencies and local groups must collaborate with juvenile and criminal justice agencies in the surveillance and sharing of information under conditions that protect the community and the civil liberties of youth.

◆ **Organizational change and development,** that is, the appropriate organization and integration of the above strategies and potential reallocation of resources among involved agencies.

Technical assistance manuals (Spergel et al., 1992b) that guide implementation of each of these components are available.[15] The model and its strategies should be designed and targeted based on a strategic problem assessment and implemented through a sequenced, empirically driven process. A steering committee comprising key community leaders and agency staff must provide overall direction and support for the implementation of the five strategies.

The OJJDP Comprehensive Gang Model embraces the concept of effective use of the social controls inherent in various social institutions. As part of this approach, individuals, families, the community as a whole, agencies, and organizations—both formal and informal—are reminded that they have a stake in supporting positive behaviors and in taking a firm stance against illegal activities, including gang crime and violence, substance abuse, and illegitimate behaviors. In practice, this means that family members, adolescents, community residents, and agency workers (including police and probation officers) must work collaboratively while carrying out their distinctive functions to ensure positive adolescent

---

[14] See Spergel et al., 1992a; Spergel et al., 1992b; Spergel, Chance, et al., 1994; Spergel, Curry, et al., 1994; see also Spergel and Curry, 1990, 1993.

[15] These manuals are available from the Juvenile Justice Clearinghouse by calling 800–638–8736.

behaviors. A summary of the five demonstration sites originally chosen to implement the model follows (Burch and Kane, 1999).

The Mesa Gang Intervention Project (Mesa, AZ). The target area for the Mesa Gang Intervention Project (MGIP) is an area of the city served by Mesa and Powell Junior High Schools. Within the target area, 18 gangs with an estimated 650 members have been identified by the Mesa Police Department. The project has targeted 125 youth who are involved in gangs or at high risk for gang involvement and who either reside in or are known to be active within the target area. Key collaborators in the project, which is overseen by a steering committee made up of agency and grassroots executives, are the city of Mesa, the Mesa Police Department, Maricopa County Adult and Juvenile Probation Departments, Prehab of Arizona, the Mesa Boys & Girls Club, Arizona State University, the United Way, and others.

A team of two gang detectives, one adult and two juvenile probation officers, a youth intervention specialist, and two full-time and two part-time street outreach workers works with and monitors the youth on a daily basis. The team is located in a storefront office within the target community. The MGIP gang detectives and probation officers provide monitoring and surveillance of youth in the program while supporting street outreach workers and staff from other community-based agencies. These staff ensure delivery of necessary services such as counseling, job referrals, drug and alcohol treatment, and other social services. The MGIP team uses a team problem-solving approach to ensure that progress is made with each youth in the program. The team also provides community assistance, including educating residents about local gang problems and hearing their concerns regarding the neighborhood. Gang education is also provided to community members through various professional, neighborhood, and civic groups within the target area.

A computer literacy lab was recently added to the MGIP office, through the support of the Arizona Superior Court. The State of Arizona recently provided additional support to the city of Mesa and MGIP for a mentoring component, and MGIP is supporting a Gang Prevention Through Targeted Outreach program at the Mesa Boys & Girls Club.

Other services provided include a cognitive restructuring class for gang-involved youth; parenting classes; services for gang-involved girls; an arts program; summer camp programming focusing on cultural diversity; and tattoo removal services following community service, an educational session, and an agreement not to get any new tattoos for 2 years. Looking toward the prospect of sustaining local support for project activities, the Mesa Police Department has shifted administrative oversight of the project to the police department's gang unit.

Tucson Gang Project (OUR Town Family Center, Tucson, AZ). The Tucson Gang Project focused on the Vistas neighborhoods on the south side of Tucson, which have approximately 4 main gangs with an estimated 350 gang members. The project served more than 100 youth. Its outreach component operated out of the local Boys & Girls Club in the target area. The primary partners in the project included the Tucson Police Department, Pima County juvenile probation and parole, the Tucson Unified School District, the Tucson Boys & Girls Club, Quail Enterprises (a research and evaluation firm), and a treatment agency known as La Fontera. The project collaborated with, received referrals from, and made referrals to a number of other local agencies. Street outreach workers, probation officers, a police gang unit officer, and others worked to provide services and opportunities on a daily basis to youth targeted by the project and held them accountable for their negative behavior using a range of graduated sanctions. Weekly staff meetings with other agency representatives were supplemented by weekly meetings among project team members to review client and community progress and needs. A community mobilizer on the project staff worked with community agencies and residents of the target neighborhood to keep attention focused on gang issues and completed a community member survey on the gang problem. The Gang Prevention Through Targeted Outreach program was integrated into the project's overall strategy and focused on younger at-risk youth. Where possible, staff from other programs joined gang project staff meetings to share information and coordinate efforts. Project staffing was supplemented by the use of AmeriCorps volunteers.

Although Federal funding for this project has ended, project partners including OUR Town, Quail Enterprises, and the Pima County Juvenile Probation

Department are continuing their collaboration and are providing services to project youth through local and other Federal support.

Riverside's Comprehensive Community-Wide Approach to Gang Prevention, Intervention, and Suppression (Riverside, CA, Police Department). The Riverside project is focused on two communities known to be high gang-crime areas. Twenty-one gangs with approximately 1,230 members exist in these communities. Currently, more than 150 gang-involved and high-risk youth are targeted by the project. The project is guided by a steering committee comprising local agencies and organizations, including the Riverside County Juvenile Court, the Riverside County District Attorney's Office,[16] the Riverside County and Alvord Unified School Districts, the Youth Service Center, and other agency and community leaders.

Although the lead agency is the Riverside Police Department, key support is provided by Riverside County Probation, the Youth Service Center, the City of Riverside Human Resources Department, the University of California at Riverside, and many other local agencies. Outreach workers and area social service agencies aid project youth daily, and police and probation officers work to keep youth from becoming involved in criminal or delinquent activities. Outreach workers and other service agencies discuss service needs during weekly meetings, and area safety, gang activities, and accountability issues during biweekly meetings with police and probation officers. Youth are encouraged to attend these meetings, are supported in attending school, and are provided job training, opportunities for regular employment, and social services. Probation officers and police carry out home visits, area surveillance, arrests, and other controls. The project has been enhanced by the probation department's development of youth accountability boards in Riverside and by a new school-based outreach program that will provide services to youth at risk of gang involvement.

The Riverside gang project also involves a job training component conducted by the city's Human Resources

Department. If youth cannot be placed immediately into ongoing employment programs in the city, they are eligible for the project's 40-hour job training program. The program consists of job readiness training (covering issues such as résumé/application writing, proper attitudes, leadership skills, communication, and cultural differences) and a job stipend for completing on-the-job training through temporary employment with local agencies and companies. The program gives youth the skills they need to seek job opportunities, apply, and be selected. It gives employers a chance to give back to the community while they gain subsidized staff. The program also works to place youth into permanent employment and provides followup once they are employed.

Bloomington/Normal's Comprehensive Community-Wide Approach to Gang Prevention, Intervention, and Suppression (Project OZ, Inc., Bloomington, IL). Although all of Bloomington and Normal, IL, were included in its target area, in which 8 gangs with 640 members were known to exist, this project dealt mainly with youth from the City of Bloomington. Along with the Bloomington and Normal Police Departments, the McLean County Juvenile Court, juvenile probation, the Bloomington and Normal schools, the Western Avenue Community Center, the Bloomington Boys & Girls Club, the McLean County State's Attorney, and other agencies focused on gang-involved and at-risk youth in Bloomington and Normal by providing support, suppression, and intervention services and opportunities such as job training and placement. Regular staff meetings for outreach workers were supplemented with biweekly meetings with the Bloomington Police Department's proactive unit, adult and juvenile probation, juvenile parole, and a school resource officer to review the progress of project youth, special problems in the cities, and overall gang activities. Outreach workers assisted project youth who were in the community and project youth who were incarcerated but expected to be released in the near future. The project was enhanced by an OJJDP mentoring grant that provided services to community youth at risk of gang membership and by a local business owned and operated by the project's steering committee that served as a job training site and the project's job development office. State Farm Insurance, which is

---

[16] The prosecution component of this program is described in Johnson, Webster, and Conners, 1995.

headquartered in Bloomington, also provided tremendous support to the project, and the Boys & Girls Clubs' Gang Prevention Through Targeted Outreach program was integrated into the project and focused on youth at high risk for gang involvement.

Although OJJDP support has ended, aspects of the project are continuing through other Federal, State, and local support.

San Antonio's Gang Rehabilitation, Assessment, and Services Program (San Antonio, TX, Police Department). The Gang Rehabilitation, Assessment, and Services Program's (GRAASP's) target community was located on the southwest side of San Antonio. The program identified a target population of 100 gang-involved youth from the area's 15 gangs and 1,664 gang members. In addition to the San Antonio Police Department, key partners in GRAASP included the Bexar County Department of Probation, the Texas Youth Commission (TYC), the San Antonio Unified School District, the University of Texas at San Antonio, Cellular On Patrol (COP—a citizens' crime watch group), and other community agencies and grassroots groups. Street-based outreach workers employed by the city of San Antonio worked together with other social service agencies, a job developer, probation officers, city police officers assigned to community policing and tactical units, TYC staff, and others. Coordination and case management meetings were held regularly with outreach workers. Police and probation officers were included if issues arose, although communication between police, probation, and other GRAASP staff also took place outside of regular meetings. The project coordinator, outreach staff, and job developer worked together in an office near the target area. The project supported graffiti paint-outs (i.e., graffiti cleanup), community health fairs, recreational opportunities for project youth, and other community development activities in conjunction with local neighborhood associations. As OJJDP funding has ended, local political leaders from the target area have been working with project agencies to determine ways of sustaining some of the project's strategies and services.

Many lessons have been learned in each of these sites that are expected to greatly enhance the Nation's knowledge about responding to chronic and emerging youth gang problems in both large and small communities. A University of Chicago evaluation of the demonstration effort is expected to shed light on what did and did not work in each site. In addition, the evaluation will inform OJJDP and the field as to how promising the Comprehensive Community-Wide Approach to Gang Prevention, Intervention, and Suppression may be in dealing with youth gang crime and violence. While final results are not expected until 2001, anecdotal and preliminary outcome data suggest that these projects have been successful in reducing gang crime and increasing prosocial opportunities such as special school training and job programs.

The Gang Violence Reduction Program

A variation of the comprehensive model Spergel and his colleagues designed was implemented in the Little Village neighborhood of Chicago, a low-income and working-class community that is approximately 90 percent Mexican American (Spergel and Grossman, 1997). Called the Gang Violence Reduction Program, it was administered by the Chicago Police Department. The program targeted mainly older members (ages 17 to 24) of two of the area's most violent Hispanic gangs, the Latin Kings and the Two Six. It is important to note that the program targeted and provided services to youth involved with

Ebb and Flow of Gang Violence

Decker (1996) delineates a seven-step process that accounts for the peaks and valleys in levels of gang violence. The process begins with a loosely organized gang:

1. Gang members feel loose bonds to the gang.

2. Gang members collectively perceive a threat from a rival gang (which increases gang cohesion).

3. A mobilizing event occurs—possibly, but not necessarily, violent.

4. Activity escalates.

5. One of the gangs lashes out in violence.

6. Violence and activity rapidly deescalate.

7. The other gang retaliates.

these two gangs, rather than to the gangs as groups. These two gangs accounted for about 70 percent of serious gang violence in the Little Village community.

The Gang Violence Reduction Program consisted mainly of two coordinated strategies: (1) targeted control of violent or potentially violent youth gang offenders in the form of increased supervision and suppression by the probation department and police and (2) provision of a wide range of social services and opportunities for targeted youth to encourage their transition to legitimate behavior through education, jobs, job training, family support, and brief counseling. The program was staffed by tactical police officers, probation officers, community youth workers from the target neighborhood, and workers in Neighbors Against Gang Violence, a community organization established to support the project. This organization was composed of representatives from local churches, a job placement agency, youth service agencies, other community groups, the alderman's office, and local citizens. The program incorporated a comprehensive set of integrated and coordinated strategies: suppression, social intervention, opportunities provision, and community mobilization.

Evaluation results, covering 3 out of 5 years of program operations, were positive (Spergel and Grossman, 1997; Spergel, Grossman, and Wa, 1998; Thornberry and Burch, 1997). Favorable results included a lower level of serious gang violence among the targeted gang members than among members of comparable gangs in the area, who had been exposed to a traditional approach based mainly on suppression. Specifically, there were fewer arrests for serious gang crimes (especially aggravated batteries and aggravated assaults) involving members of targeted gangs in comparison with a control group of youth from the same gangs and members of other gangs in Little Village. It appears that the coordinated project approach, using a combination of various social interventions involving youth outreach workers[17] and suppression tactics, was more

effective with more violent youth, while the sole use of youth workers was more effective with less violent youth. Social interventions included counseling, crisis intervention, gang homicide intervention, job placement, and family, school, and special education programs and services. There also was notable improvement in residents' perceptions of gang crime and police effectiveness in dealing with that crime. The Illinois Criminal Justice Information Authority (1999:4) concluded that "the project appears to have been a success" and that "the cohesive team approach was probably at the heart of the project's success in reducing gang crime, particularly gang violence."

Comprehensive Strategy for Serious, Violent, and Chronic Juvenile Offenders

Gang membership is one of the strongest predictors of individual violence in adolescence (Hawkins et al., 1998). In the Rochester site of OJJDP's Program of Research on the Causes and Correlates of Delinquency, gang members committed nearly twice as many delinquent acts as nonmembers (see figure 1), and two-thirds of chronic violent offenders were gang members for a time (Thornberry, Huizinga, and Loeber, 1995). OJJDP's Comprehensive Strategy for Serious, Violent, and Chronic Juvenile Offenders (see Wilson and Howell, 1993) provides a framework for strategic community planning and program development targeting serious, violent, and chronic juvenile offenders. Given the overlap of risk factors for gang participation with those for nongang serious and violent offending (Howell, 1998b), the Comprehensive Strategy offers an effective community mobilization and planning model for responding to the problem of gang activity.[18]

The OJJDP Comprehensive Strategy organizes programs in a framework composed of three main components: prevention, early intervention, and graduated sanctions. The graduated sanctions component consists of a system of sanctions, including

---

[17] Six requirements guided outreach workers' daily activities: operate as part of a team structure, continually assess the gang and gang member situation in the community, focus on social intervention and social opportunities provision, work with the community to achieve gang violence reduction, deal with police harassment of gang members, and cope with outreach performance tasks (Spergel, 1999).

---

[18] The *Guide for Implementing the Comprehensive Strategy for Serious, Violent, and Chronic Juvenile Offenders* (Howell, 1995) is a resource for carrying out the OJJDP Comprehensive Strategy.

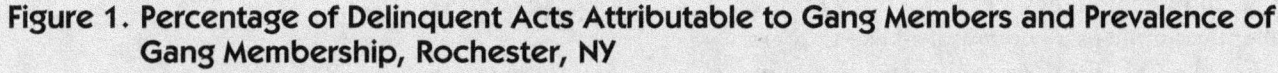

Figure 1. Percentage of Delinquent Acts Attributable to Gang Members and Prevalence of Gang Membership, Rochester, NY

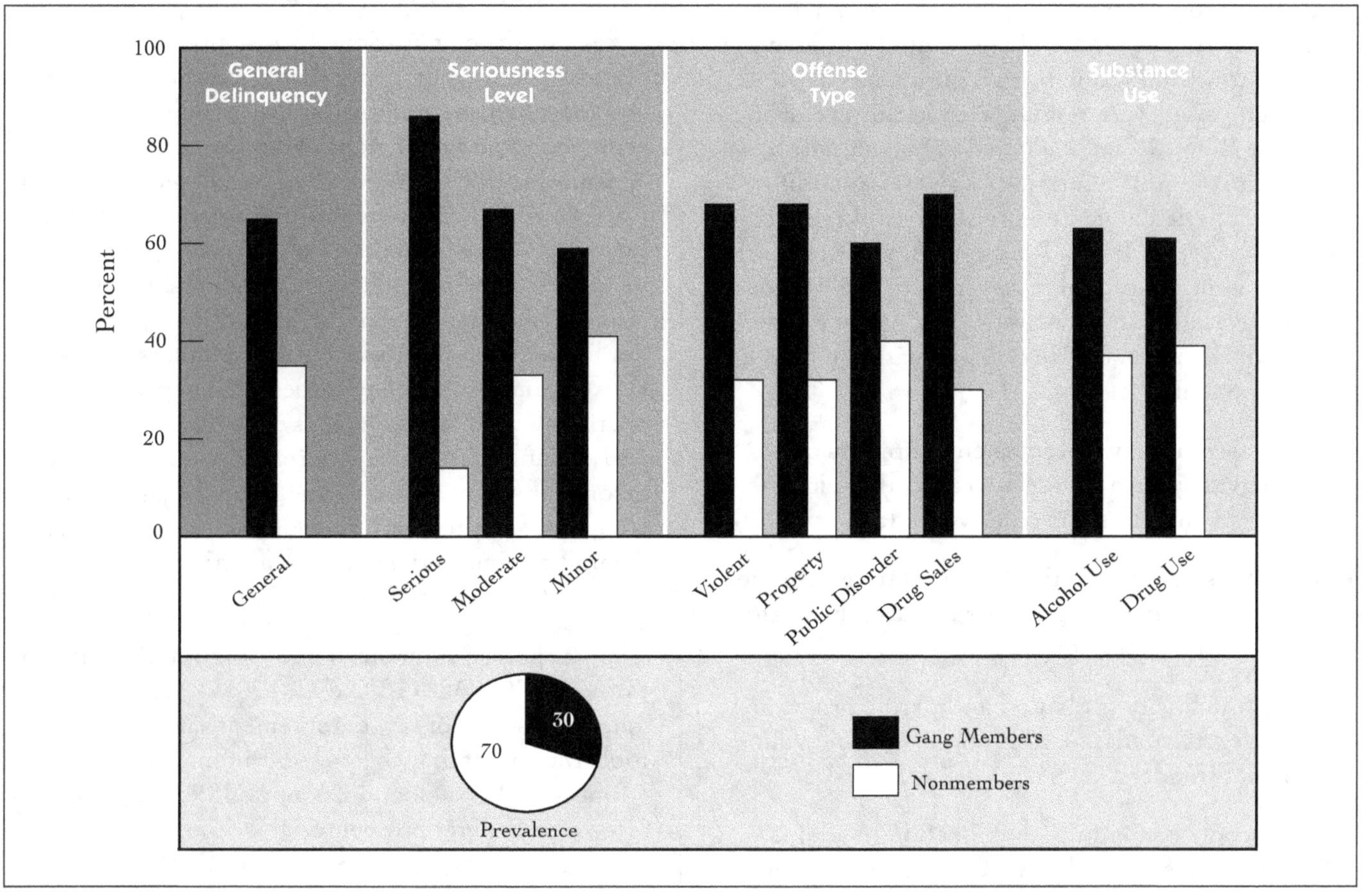

[Figure: Bar chart showing Percent (y-axis, 0 to 100) across four groupings. Bars compare Gang Members (black) and Nonmembers (white).

General Delinquency:
- General: Gang Members ~65, Nonmembers ~35

Seriousness Level:
- Serious: Gang Members ~86, Nonmembers ~14
- Moderate: Gang Members ~67, Nonmembers ~33
- Minor: Gang Members ~59, Nonmembers ~41

Offense Type:
- Violent: Gang Members ~68, Nonmembers ~32
- Property: Gang Members ~68, Nonmembers ~32
- Public Disorder: Gang Members ~60, Nonmembers ~40
- Drug Sales: Gang Members ~70, Nonmembers ~30

Substance Use:
- Alcohol Use: Gang Members ~63, Nonmembers ~37
- Drug Use: Gang Members ~61, Nonmembers ~39

Pie chart (Prevalence): 30 (black), 70 (white)

Legend: Gang Members (black), Nonmembers (white)]

Source: Thornberry and Burch, 1997.

arrest, adjudication, intensive probation, incarceration, and aftercare for juvenile offenders, along with a continuum of rehabilitation options. One such option is found in the use of multisystemic therapy, which has been shown to be highly effective with serious, violent, and chronic juvenile offenders (Henggeler, 1997). It is currently being tested in Galveston, TX, in the Second Chance program, which targets gang-involved youth (Thomas, 1996).

Two other programs illustrate how graduated sanctions may be effective with gang members. In its Early Intervention Program, the Orange County (CA) Probation Department targets potential (under age 15) serious, violent, and chronic offenders, for whom gang involvement is one risk factor. Preliminary results show a 50-percent reduction in recidivism as a result of using probation and other sanctions with a wide

range of treatment interventions for both offenders and their families (Schumacher and Kurz, 2000).[19] Intensive probation and other more restrictive suppression measures, including criminal prosecution, are used with older, hardcore gang members in the TARGET program described earlier in this Summary. The Early Intervention Program uses a continuum of sanctions and service options for the potential serious and violent offenders it targets.

The Baton Rouge, LA, Partnership for the Prevention of Juvenile Gun Violence (Office of Juvenile

---

[19] The California legislature recently appropriated funds for replication and testing of the program in six other counties within the State. In addition, it is being replicated in McLean County, IL, in a collaborative project involving the Illinois Attorney General's Gang Crime Prevention Center and the county's Department of Court Services.

Justice and Delinquency Prevention, 1999) is an excellent example of a community-based program that uses the OJJDP Comprehensive Strategy framework to prevent and reduce adolescent violence. This strategy quite likely would be effective in preventing and reducing gang problems as well. Although gangs were not targeted in this program (because Baton Rouge did not have a gang problem at the time of implementation), other communities that are experiencing gang problems could replicate the steps taken in Baton Rouge. The partnership targeted multiple-offender youth up to age 21 from two high-crime ZIP code areas. The partnership designed a comprehensive strategy with the following components:

◆ A multiagency law enforcement (suppression) strategy to reduce gun-related and other violent crimes by juveniles and older youth (ages 17 to 20).

◆ An intensive intervention program to reduce the risk factors for the highest risk youth, their families, and the community.

◆ A high-intensity probation and parole program that targets an identified group of chronic young violent offenders.

◆ Grassroots community mobilization to address the problems of hard-to-reach families and the highest risk youth.

◆ A long-range prevention program that identifies, links, and strengthens existing resources to serve youth who may be at risk.

Baton Rouge police arrest data show that the number of juveniles arrested for all crimes dropped more than 27 percent between 1997 and 1998 and there was a 21-percent decline in the number arrested for violent crimes or drug offenses.[20]

---

[20] Yvonne L. Day, Baton Rouge Partnership for the Prevention of Juvenile Gun Violence, personal communication, October 15, 1999.

Legislation

Federal and State Legislation

Arrest for the commission of substantive criminal offenses, defined by Federal or State statute, is the main mechanism used by law enforcement to prosecute youth and adult gangs (Bureau of Justice Assistance, 1997b). Innovative penalty enhancement provisions that complement substantive criminal code provisions have been developed for use against gang members. They provide enhanced punishment for crimes that are often gang related, although they are not limited in application to gang members. These laws not only enhance penalties against principals charged with offenses such as drug trafficking, homicide, assault with a weapon, robbery, home invasion, arson, extortion, and auto theft, but also against accomplices charged with such offenses as conspiracy to commit a crime and aiding and abetting overt criminal acts (Bureau of Justice Assistance, 1997b).

The Racketeer Influenced and Corrupt Organizations (RICO) Act (18 U.S.C. 1961 et seq.) "has emerged as one of law enforcement's most effective tools for combating organized criminal activity" (Johnson, Webster, and Connors, 1995:7). Used most often as a Federal prosecutorial weapon against high-ranking criminal group members, RICO has been used against youth and adult gang members by 17 percent of local prosecutors in large counties and less than 10 percent of prosecutors in small counties. The Institute for Law and Justice (ILJ) survey of local prosecutors' approaches to youth and adult gang prosecution revealed that "traditional criminal law can reach most gang crime. Existing laws in most jurisdictions also may allow more options for prosecution than statutes specifically aimed at gang members and crimes" (Johnson, Webster, and Connors, 1995:7). In 14 States, prosecutors reported charging street gangs with violations of new, specialized gang offenses. Prosecutors in the other 36 States indicated that they had filed charges against street gangs under existing substantive provisions of their criminal codes. However, some common gang offenses, such as defacing property with graffiti, are often not addressed by State criminal codes, but rather by municipal ordinances.

Some jurisdictions charge youth and adult gang leaders involved in criminal enterprises (e.g., crack cocaine networks) with aiding and abetting (Bureau of Justice Assistance, 1997b). Thus, a gang leader convicted of aiding and abetting may be punished as a principal in the criminal enterprise. Similarly, when gang members participate in the preliminary stages of a crime (e.g., riding in a car to the crime scene), but do not actually participate in the crime itself, they increase the likelihood of being convicted of aiding and abetting.

The ILJ survey (Johnson, Webster, and Connors, 1995), as discussed earlier, found that 14 States have recently enacted new code provisions addressing youth and adult gangs. California, Florida, Georgia, Illinois, Louisiana, and Nevada have enhanced penalties for crimes carried out in participation with or at the direction of gangs. The California Street Terrorism, Enforcement, and Prevention (STEP) Act of 1988 (California Penal Code § 186.22) has served as a model emulated by Florida, Georgia, Illinois, Louisiana, and other jurisdictions. A unique notification process is used to inform persons that they can be prosecuted under STEP (Klein, 1995a). Police and/or prosecutors gather evidence that a targeted gang fits the STEP Act's definition. This information is presented to the court, resulting in a judicial order. Gang members are then notified in writing that they are known members of such a group. Following such notice, the Act can then be applied to these members, enhancing penalties for subsequent offenses because of the commission of crimes while involved in a gang. Some law enforcement sources indicate that these provisions may be partly responsible for the recent trend of gang members concealing their membership status, thus making it more difficult to identify or "certify" their status for purposes of these provisions.

Although suppression has been a predominant theme in new gang legislation over the past few years, a number of States have enacted new youth gang prevention measures (Hunzeker, 1993; see also Johnson, Webster, and Connors, 1995). For example, the State of Washington enacted a Youth Gang Reduction Act in 1991 that seeks to prevent elementary and secondary students from joining gangs.

Hawaii has created a new program that combines suppression and prevention strategies. Hardcore gang criminals are prosecuted, whereas the growth of gangs is addressed through prevention and education efforts focused on younger juveniles. The results of a process evaluation of Hawaii's Youth Gang Response System have been consistently positive (Chesney-Lind et al., 1992, 1995a, 1995b, 1999).

City Ordinances and Court Injunctions

Cities have enacted a number of measures that restrict or prohibit youth and adult gang activities, such as banning gang member use of public parks that have been gang confrontation sites and prohibiting cruising and numerous forms of belligerent public behavior (National Crime Prevention Council, 1996; Pyle, 1995). Other cities have attempted to discourage gang membership by prohibiting behavior that manifests gang membership, including wearing gang colors, flashing gang signs, and communicating gang membership or insults to other gangs. Housing authorities are authorized by HUD to evict gang members caught possessing or using guns (National Crime Prevention Council, 1996). In one case, the Chicago Housing Authority (CHA), in conjunction with the Chicago Police Department, implemented a program called Operation Clean Sweep (OCS) that gained temporary control of numerous buildings (Bureau of Justice Assistance, 1997b). The facilities were then secured by CHA. In the next phase, property management was improved and, following an assessment, social services were provided to residents who needed them. HUD is studying the benefits of the OCS approach.

Unlike nuisance abatement laws under which local jurisdictions seek court injunctions against continuing nuisances on behalf of the public, private nuisance actions are initiated by the aggrieved party to obtain specific individual relief from gang activities (Bureau of Justice Assistance, 1998). Some cities have expanded their use of nuisance abatement laws to restrict youth and adult gang member activities (Bureau of Justice Assistance, 1997b; Los Angeles City Attorney Gang Prosecution Section, 1995). If property is involved, nuisance abatement relief ranges from stopping gangs from using particular properties in criminal activity to providing for forfeiture of property used in criminal activity. For example, a Colorado law permits forfeiture of cars used in drive-by shootings (Bureau of Justice Assistance, 1997b). Civil remedies also have been used to deal with gang and drug situations.[21]

In 1992, Chicago, IL, officials adopted the Gang Congregation Ordinance, an antiloitering law targeted at street gangs. It reads in part: "Whenever a police officer observes a person whom he reasonably believes to be a criminal street gang member loitering in any public place with one or more other persons, he shall order all such persons to disperse and remove themselves from the area. Any person who does not promptly obey such an order is in violation of this order."[22]

In 1993, Jesus Morales and other individuals were charged with violating the Chicago ordinance. They petitioned Cook County Circuit Court to dismiss the charges, arguing that the Gang Congregation Ordinance is unconstitutional and violates their rights under the 1st, 4th, and 14th amendments of the U.S. Constitution. The circuit court granted their motion and dismissed the charges. The city appealed. An Illinois appellate court upheld the circuit court ruling and the State Supreme Court affirmed, saying that the Gang Congregation Ordinance was vague, discriminatory, and a violation of the right to free assembly. In 1998, the City of Chicago appealed to the U.S. Supreme Court, which affirmed the original ruling[23] that found the ordinance to be unconstitutional. This decision has caused other jurisdictions with similar laws to reconsider. In one Chicago suburb, the city has instead adopted an ordinance that allows police to confiscate the vehicles of persons in violation of a city-imposed curfew. This ordinance may also face judicial scrutiny.

Also in 1993, the Los Angeles County District Attorney sought (and was granted) an injunction to ban the Blythe Street Gang from congregating in public areas (American Civil Liberties Union, 1997; Hoffman and Silverstein, 1995). The district attorney asserted that this Hispanic gang, some 500 strong, had virtually transformed a quiet San Fernando Valley neighborhood into an occupied zone. Innocent residents were said to be held captive in their own apartments. Since 1993, about a dozen California cities have requested or received similar court injunctions. In 1997, the California Supreme Court upheld this gang suppression tactic. However, an evaluation by the American Civil Liberties Union of the impact of the Blythe Street Gang injunction questioned its effectiveness, finding that violent crime and drug trafficking actually increased following the injunction (American Civil Liberties Union, 1997).

Juvenile curfew. Curfew ordinances also are being used to thwart gang activity. Long Beach, CA, officials established a 10 p.m. to 6 a.m. curfew ordinance directed at gang members. Although city officials acknowledge the possible displacement of offenses outside the curfew period, a significant reduction in gang-related crimes during the curfew period has been observed (Pratcher, 1994).

Even though curfew laws are not new, they have come to be seen as an ideal means of dealing with youth gangs and violent juvenile crime (Hemmens and Bennett, 1999). One review found that 59 out of 77 cities with populations in excess of 200,000 had juvenile curfew ordinances by 1994 (Ruefle and Reynolds, 1995), and approximately 1,000 local curfew ordinances have been adopted since 1990 (Shepherd, 1996). Curfew ordinances have been challenged on constitutional grounds, including the rights to free assembly; equal protection against unreasonable stopping and detainment; due process; privacy, including the right to family autonomy; and to not be deprived of liberty without due process (LeBoeuf, 1996). The main objections, however, are on the grounds that curfews violate the equal protection clause of the fourth amendment "by setting up a suspect classification based on age, and that they result in selective enforcement to the detriment of minority youth" (Ruefle and Reynolds, 1995:349).

To pass constitutional muster, laws that impinge on fundamental constitutional rights undergo strict scrutiny. Jurisdictions must (1) demonstrate

---

[21] See Bureau of Justice Assistance (1998), pp. 174–182, for examples in Berkeley, CA; Joliet, IL; and San Diego, CA.

[22] Chicago Municipal Code § 8–4–05 (June 17, 1992).

[23] *City of Chicago* v. *Morales*, 119 S. Ct. 1849 (1999). The U.S. Supreme Court said such restrictive laws should spell out what illegal activity would trigger an arrest.

that there is a compelling State interest and (2) narrowly tailor the means to achieve the law's objective (LeBoeuf, 1996). The Dallas, TX, curfew ordinance, described in more detail on page 24, has been held by the Federal court to satisfy these requirements (see LeBoeuf, 1996:4–5, for further information). However, this ruling neither guarantees protection from future constitutional legal challenges to the ordinance as violating provisions of the U.S. Constitution or State constitutions nor forecloses challenges based on nonconstitutional grounds (LeBoeuf, 1996; see also Hemmens and Bennett, 1999, for a review of State and Federal cases challenging juvenile curfews).

Hemmens and Bennett (1999) observe that "there is remarkably little empirical research on the impact of curfews on either juvenile crime or the overall crime rate; thus, it is unclear how effective they are at reducing crime." In the single study that has examined the effectiveness of curfews on gang crime, an evaluation of the Dallas curfew law found that police use of aggressive curfew and truancy enforcement in concert appeared to reduce violent gang crimes (Fritsch, Caeti, and Taylor, 1999). Some displacement of gang crime into areas of the city with a smaller law enforcement presence was observed. Researchers concluded, however, that this displacement appeared to be minimal.

A Detroit curfew study (Hunt and Weiner, 1977) showed more significant displacement, finding that in the afternoon, juvenile crime increased by 13 percent during the study period while dropping by 6 percent during curfew hours. Nevertheless, curfew enforcement may be an effective police suppression strategy, particularly if combined with truancy enforcement and targeting of specific gangs in small geographic areas.

Further evaluation of curfew enforcement is needed, especially taking into account possible displacement effects. Additional research is also needed on police targeting of particular gangs in specific localities. This may well have been a key element in the success of the Dallas antigang initiative (see page 24), given that seven of the city's most violent gangs operated in the target area. Another issue that must be examined is whether adults or juveniles are responsible for most violent gang-related crime. The Dallas study did not examine the extent of the overall drop in reported violent gang-related crime among juveniles versus young adults. The 1996 National Youth Gang Survey revealed that young adult gang members (age 18 and older) are relatively more prevalent in jurisdictions that report higher degrees of gang member involvement in violent crimes (aggravated assault and robbery) (National Youth Gang Center, 1999; see also Wiebe, Meeker, and Vila, in press).

Assessment of Youth Gang Programs

In 1988, with OJJDP support, Spergel and his colleagues conducted a nationwide assessment of youth gang prevention, intervention, and suppression programs (Spergel, 1995; Spergel and Curry, 1993; Spergel, Curry, et al., 1994). The assessment included a survey of 254 respondents in 45 communities and 6 special program sites regarding strategies they employed and their perception of which were the most effective. All surveyed sites had youth gang problems and organized responses to those problems. Responses were categorized into the major program types that Spergel (1991) identified in a literature review of gang programs: community organization, social intervention, provision of opportunities, and suppression. The survey team added a fifth response category: organizational change and development.

Suppression was the most frequently employed strategy (44 percent), followed by social intervention (31 percent), organizational change and development (11 percent), community organization (9 percent), and provision of opportunities (5 percent). Survey respondents believed different approaches were effective in chronic (longstanding) versus emerging (more recent) gang problem cities (Spergel and Curry, 1990, 1993). Provision of social opportunities[24] was perceived to be more effective in sites with chronic gang problems. Community organization (mobilization)[25] was believed to be an effective strategy, but only when social opportunities were also provided. In

contrast, respondents in cities with emerging gang problems saw community organization (mobilization) as the most effective strategy. Overall, respondents were not confident that their antigang efforts were particularly effective in reducing gang problems. Only 23 percent of the police and 10 percent of all other respondents believed their community's gang situation improved between 1980 and 1987. By 1998, the National Youth Gang Survey revealed a more optimistic view among law enforcement agencies (see figure 2).

Assessments of gang programs by law enforcement agencies show that suppression programs remain very popular, but that other approaches are gaining acceptance. In the course of a national gang migration study (Maxson, Woods, and Klein, 1995), respondents in about one-fourth of the 211 cities

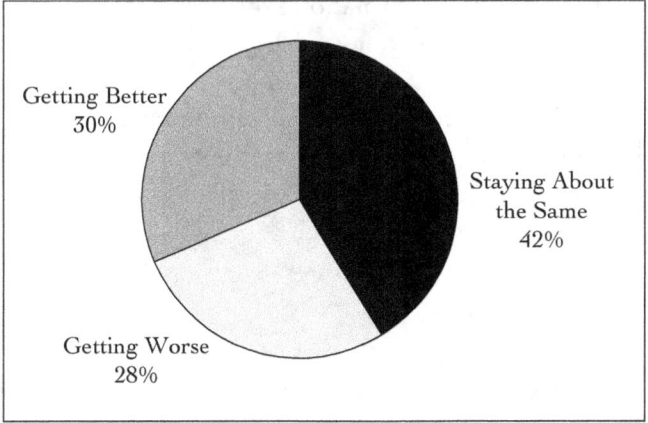

Figure 2. Law Enforcement Agencies' Perception of Youth Gang Problems, 1998

Getting Better 30%

Staying About the Same 42%

Getting Worse 28%

Source: Moore and Cook, 1999.

---

[24] This includes job preparation, training, placement, and development and assistance with school problems, tutoring, and education of youth gang members.

[25] This includes involvement of local citizens, including former gang youth and current gang influentials, community groups, and agencies and coordination of programs and staff functions across agencies.

surveyed were asked to assess the use and effectiveness of several gang policies and practices in reducing the volume or negative impact of gang migrants on their cities (see table 3). Most respondents said coordination with Federal, State, and local law enforcement agencies was relatively common, but few law enforcement officers viewed this as effective in reducing gang migration or illegal activities. Three-fourths of the surveyed departments targeted violations of selected laws (e.g., narcotics laws), but only 42 percent of them viewed this strategy as effective. Enforcement of specific gang laws (e.g., the Street Terrorism Enforcement Act) was not viewed as a particularly effective response. About 40 percent of the surveyed law enforcement agencies used gang sweeps and other suppression strategies (44 percent), which were said to be effective by a majority of officers. Almost two-thirds of the surveyed cities employed community collaboration strategies, and more than half (54 percent) believed these to be effective. In sum, the strategies perceived to be effective by a majority of law enforcement respondents were community collaboration (information exchange or gang awareness education) (54 percent), crime prevention activities (56 percent), and street sweeps (62 percent) or other suppression tactics (63 percent).

In addition to conducting a survey, Spergel and colleagues reviewed gang research on a variety of topics, including definitions, the nature and causes of the gang phenomenon, and the effectiveness of program strategies used by various agencies and organizations in communities. Although conclusive evaluations of these strategies are still needed, the following common elements appear to be associated with a sustained reduction of gang problems:

◆ Community leaders recognize the presence of gangs and seek to understand the nature and extent of the local gang problem through a comprehensive and systematic assessment of the gang problem.

◆ The combined leadership of the justice system and the community focuses on the mobilization of institutional and community resources to address gang problems.

Table 3. Law Enforcement Strategies and Perceived Effectiveness*

Strategy	Used	Judged Effective (if used)
Some or a lot of use		
Targeting entry points	14%	17%
Gang laws	40	19
Selected violations	76	42
Out-of-State information exchange	53	16
In-State information exchange	90	17
In-city information exchange	55	18
Federal agency operational coordination	40	16
State agency operational coordination	50	13
Local agency operational coordination	78	16
Community collaboration	64	54
Any use		
Street sweeps	40%	62%
Other suppression tactics	44	63
Crime prevention activities	15	56

* Percentage of cities, n=211. The number of cities responding to each question varied slightly.
Source: Maxson, Woods, and Klein, 1995.

◆ Those in principal roles develop a consensus —
based on problem assessment rather than
assumptions — on definitions (e.g., gang, gang
incident), specific targets of agency and interagency efforts, and interrelated strategies. Prevention and intervention efforts are focused on
the population and/or community areas in which
youth are at greatest risk for gang membership
and gang violence.

Recent characterizations of gangs and gang members in the National Youth Gang Survey and other
studies (Howell, 2000) suggest that jurisdictions
need to assess very carefully their particular youth
gang problem. Different data sources on gangs
and gang members may produce a different view of
the same gang phenomenon.

Unfortunately, the link between self-reported gang
involvement (using student surveys) and gang membership indicated in police arrest data has not been
clear. Curry (in press) analyzed this link. He used
self-report survey measures of gang involvement
for a population of at-risk Chicago youth in sixth
through eighth grades and delinquency and police
records (covering a 5-year period) to examine the
relationship between self-report survey measures in
early adolescence and subsequent police-recorded
delinquency and gang involvement. Almost two-
thirds (62 percent) of the sixth through eighth grad-
ers self-reported some level of gang involvement.
Among self-reported gang-involved youth, 51 percent were identified by the police as offenders in at
least one delinquent incident, and 20 percent were
identified by police as gang-related offenders.
Among self-identified gang-involved youth who also
were self-identified delinquents, 51 percent were
identified as offenders by police in at least one delinquent incident, and 27 percent were identified by
police as gang-related offenders. Conversely, of the
94 police-identified gang offenders, 56 percent were
self-identified as gang involved and delinquent in the
middle school survey. Thus, the gang problem as it
existed among the 429 Chicago middle-schoolers
was continuous over time. Remarkably, the 189 official delinquent offenders (i.e., those who were arrested for their offenses) (41 percent of the total)
accounted for 72 percent of the total offenses among
the 429 youth. More than half (56 percent) of these
offenders were identified by police as gang members, and they represented 22 percent of those who
self-reported gang involvement.

Curry produced sound evidence that survey research
and analysis of official records can be used to examine
different parts of a comprehensive community gang
problem that may indeed merit comprehensive
communitywide response strategies. He concluded
that although survey responses and official data
sources do not perfectly coincide, together they can
enhance researchers' understanding of gang activity.
He strongly suggests that gangs and gang members
profiled in student surveys do not represent a gang
problem separate from the one indicated by law enforcement data. Indeed, cumulative arrest data would
tend to profile mainly older, multiple-year gang members (see Battin-Pearson et al., 1999). These findings
support the potential effectiveness of comprehensive
community responses to gang crime problems that
link prevention, intervention, and suppression strategies. Prevention programs could target at-risk youth
(using self-reports), early intervention programs
could target youth in the early stages of gang involvement (using self-reports and official records), and
suppression strategies could target serious, violent,
and chronic offenders who are gang-involved (using
official records).

Any approach must be guided by concern not only
for safeguarding the community against gang crime,
but for providing support and supervision to present
and potential gang members in a way that contrib-
utes to their prosocial development (Spergel, Curry
et al., 1994; see also Burch and Chemers, 1997).

Stereotypes Versus Modern Youth Gangs

Youth gang members have long been stereotyped as young, inner-city, lower-class, ghetto or barrio, minority, sociopathic males (Klein, 1995a; Spergel, 1995). Traditionally, gangs have been viewed as racially and ethnically segregated, somewhat organized, and authoritatively controlled fighting groups (Miller, 1992). The predominant popular stereotype of youth gangs was modified significantly by the findings of a California study (Skolnick et al., 1988) more than a decade ago (see Klein, 1995a). These researchers contended that the two major Los Angeles gangs, the Crips and Bloods, had become highly organized and entrepreneurial and were expanding their drug trafficking operations to markets in other cities. Where drug markets appeared, so did violent crime. The typical gang member came to be viewed as a violent "superpredator" who repeatedly engaged in random violence and could not be reformed (DiIulio, 1996).

The distinguishing features of youth gangs and their members are still characterized mainly by popular media images based on traditional stereotypes and by public perceptions of the modern-day gangs conveyed in the California study, rather than by scientific knowledge. Indeed, some jurisdictions may be adapting a view of well-publicized Los Angeles gang problems to their own jurisdictions, which may not apply (Miethe and McCorkle, 1997a). Moreover, recent studies challenge the stereotypes of gangs and gang members (see especially, Best and Hutchinson, 1996; Decker, Bynum, and Weisel, 1998; Fleisher, 1995, 1998; Miethe and McCorkle, 1997b).

Gangs typically are not highly organized, at least not those in cities with emerging gang problems. Decker and colleagues (1998) compared the two gangs that police in Chicago, IL, and San Diego, CA, reported were most highly organized. They found that the Chicago gangs were far more organized than the San Diego gangs, but that "levels of organization are not necessarily linked to increased involvement in crime" (Decker, Bynum, and Weisel, 1998:408). Decker and colleagues' observation that the San Diego gangs were disorganized mirrored Sanders' (1994) deduction. The same conclusion was reached by others who studied gangs in emerging gang cities such as Denver, CO, and Cleveland and Columbus, OH (Huff, 1996, 1998); Kansas City, MO (Fleisher, 1998); Milwaukee, WI (Hagedorn, 1988); Pittsburgh, PA (Klein, 1995a); San Francisco, CA (Waldorf, 1993); Seattle, WA (Fleisher, 1995); and St. Louis, MO (Decker and Van Winkle, 1996). A new study also questions the territorial scope of large gangs in one of the most chronic gang cities. Even the largest gangs in Chicago are criminally active in a very small percentage of the city's geographical area (Block and Jones, 1999).

Other studies, particularly in emerging gang areas, have produced findings to counter the traditional stereotypes of youth gangs (Howell, 2000):

◆ The gangs, drugs, and violence connection appears to apply more to adult drug and criminal gangs than to youth gangs.

◆ The seemingly intractable connection of gangs, drugs, and violence is not as strong among youth gangs as suggested by traditional stereotypes.

◆ Relatively more young adult males than juveniles appear to be involved in the most criminal youth gangs, and they appear to be disproportionately involved in serious and violent crimes.

◆ It is not as difficult for adolescents to resist gang pressures as commonly believed. In most instances, adolescents can refuse to join gangs without reprisal.

◆ Gang members (especially marginal members) typically can leave the gang without serious consequences.

◆ At least in emerging gang areas, most adolescents do not remain in gangs for long periods of time, suggesting that members can be drawn away from gangs with attractive alternatives.

◆ Contemporary legends about gangs, especially initiation rites,[26] are without scientific basis.

◆ Modern gangs make less use of symbols, including gang names, clothing, and traditional initiation rites, than gangs of the past, and the meaning of their graffiti is sometimes murky or unclear (e.g., youth may use a mixture of different gang symbols).

◆ Modern youth gangs are based less on territory than gangs of the past.

◆ Drug franchising is not the principal driving force behind gang migration. The most common reasons to migrate (movement of members from one city to another) are social considerations, including family moves to improve the quality of life and to be near relatives and friends.

◆ More adolescents were members of gangs in the 1990's than in the past.

◆ More gangs are in suburban areas, small towns, and rural areas than in the past (see tables 4 and 5 and figure 3).

◆ There is more gang presence in schools than in the 1980's.

◆ There is more gang presence in detention and correctional facilities than in the past.

◆ Prison gangs have grown over the past two decades.

Members of modern gangs, especially in emerging gang areas, also have different characteristics than members in stereotypical gangs (Howell, 2000):

◆ Many members of modern adolescent gangs are "good kids" from respectable families with college-educated parents.

◆ White gang members are more prevalent in adolescent gangs than in the past (see figure 4).

◆ Females are more prevalent in adolescent gangs than previously reported.

◆ Gangs in suburban, small town, and rural areas have different characteristics than gangs in large cities. They include more females, Caucasians, and younger youth, and more have mixed membership.

◆ About one-third of all youth gangs have a significant mixture of racial and ethnic groups (see figure 4 for a breakdown of the race/ethnicity of gang members).

Table 4. Average Year of Gang Problem Onset, by Area Type

Area Type	Average Year of Onset
Large city	1989
Suburban county	1990
Small city	1992
Rural county	1993

Source: National Youth Gang Center, 1999.

Table 5. Average Year of Gang Problem Onset, by Region

Region	Average Year of Onset
West	1986
Midwest	1990
Northeast	1991
South	1991

Source: National Youth Gang Center, 1999.

---

[26] Debunked initiation rites include "the slasher under the car" (gang initiates hide under cars waiting to attack their victims) and "flicked headlights" (initiates drive at night without their headlights on; the first passing vehicle to flash its headlights becomes the target).

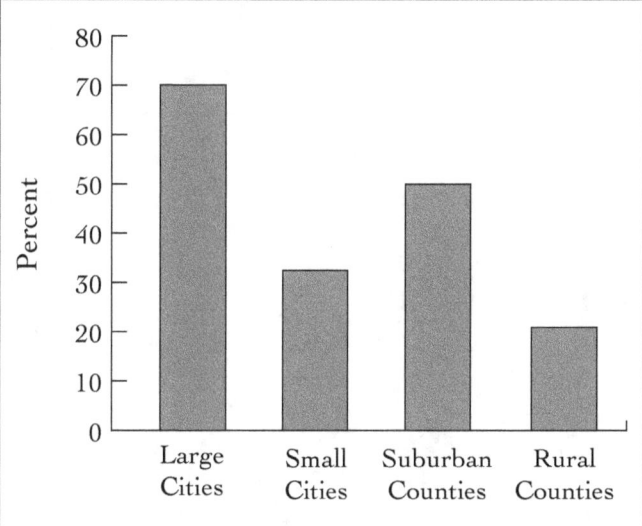

Source: Moore and Cook, 1999.

Despite these changes, youth gangs remain dangerous. Their members often engage in violence and frequently carry weapons. In an 11-city survey of eighth grade gang members, more than 90 percent of males and females had engaged in violent behavior (Deschenes and Esbensen, 1999). According to the 1998 National Youth Gang Survey, 49 percent of all respondents said that gang members used firearms in assault crimes either often or sometimes (Moore and Cook, 1999). Only 15 percent of all respondents said firearms were not used at all. Youth gangs also are beginning to age. In 1996, law enforcement agencies estimated that approximately half of their gang members were juveniles (under age 18) and half were young adults (18 and older) (National Youth Gang Center, 1999). In 1998, approximately 60 percent of the gang members were estimated to be young adults and only 40 percent were juveniles (Moore and Cook, 1999) (see figure 5). Should this trend continue, youth gangs could become more violent because it appears that adult gang members engage in more serious and violent crimes than juvenile gang members (Howell and Gleason, 1999; National Youth Gang Center, in press; Parsons and Meeker, 1999; Wiebe, Meeker, and Vila, in press).

Figure 4. Race/Ethnicity of Gang Members (Weighted for Number of Gang Members), 1998

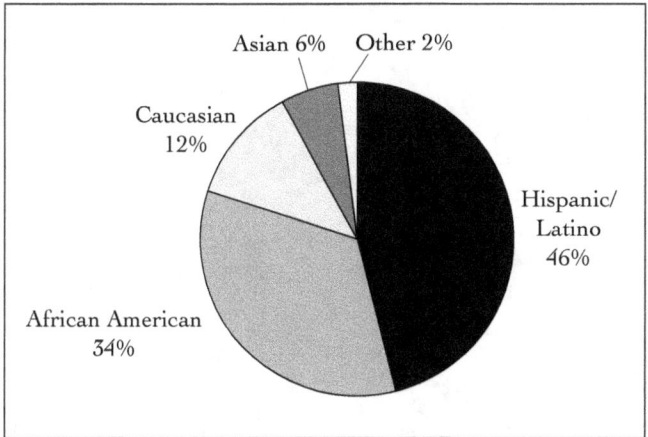

Source: Moore and Cook, 1999.

Figure 5. Age of Gang Members (Weighted for Number of Gang Members), 1998

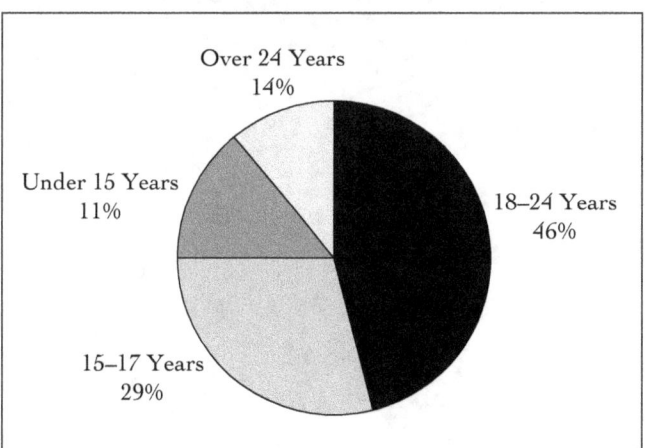

Source: Moore and Cook, 1999.

Recommendations

The literature and programs reviewed for this Summary (including sources in table 1, pages 3–4) suggest the following principles for effective youth gang programs and strategies:

◆ Both denial of gang problems and overreaction to them are detrimental to the development of effective community responses to gangs. Denial that gang problems exist precludes early intervention efforts. Overreaction in the form of excessive police force and publicizing of gangs may inadvertently serve to increase a gang's cohesion, facilitate its expansion, and lead to more crime.

◆ Community responses to gangs must begin with a thorough assessment of the specific characteristics of the gangs themselves, crimes they commit, other problems they present, and localities they affect. To conduct a thorough assessment, communities should look at community perceptions and available data. Data from law enforcement sources such as local gang and general crime data are critical. Other data should be collected from probation officers, schools, community-based youth agencies, prosecutors, and community residents. No assumptions about presumed gang problems or needed responses should be made before conducting a careful assessment.

◆ Because gang problems vary from one community to another, police, courts, corrections, and community agencies often need assistance from gang experts in assessing their gang problem(s) and in developing appropriate and measured responses.

◆ Law enforcement agents view suppression tactics (e.g., street sweeps, intensified surveillance, hotspot targeting, and caravanning), crime prevention activities, and community collaboration—

in that order—as most effective in preventing and controlling gang crime. Targeting specific gang crimes, locations, gangs, and gang members appears to be the most effective suppression tactic; therefore, police increasingly adhere to the mantra: "Investigate the crime; not the culture."[27]

◆ Long-term proactive investigations of entire gangs are more effective than short-term, reactive investigations of individual gang members. According to Jackson and McBride (1985:28), "Gang crimes are viewed by specialists as more dangerous than other crimes because they are not isolated acts, but links in a chain of events that must be broken."

◆ Each city's gang program should be supported by a gang information system that provides sound and current crime incident data that can be linked to gang members and used to enhance police and other agency interventions. At a minimum, law enforcement agencies must ensure that gang crimes are coded separately from nongang crimes so that these events can be tracked, studied, and analyzed to support more efficient and effective antigang strategies.

◆ The success of the Gang Violence Reduction Program in Chicago's Little Village neighborhood has demonstrated the effectiveness of multiagency coordination and integration among youth services (including street outreach), police, probation, parole, grassroots organizations, and corrections in controlling and redirecting serious and violent gang members. Preliminary positive

---

[27] This principle is attributed to Sergeant David Starbuck, Gang Squad, Kansas City Police Department, Kansas City, MO. Personal communication, March 31, 2000.

results from other multiagency programs provide further encouragement that serious and violent youth gang crime can be controlled, if not reduced. Narrower strategies, such as combining police and probation surveillance, have also shown some promise but have not yet been evaluated rigorously.

◆ Systematic assessment of gang problems in the juvenile and criminal justice systems is needed, including the connections between prison gangs and youth gangs. Nearly 9 in 10 juvenile detention facilities have gang members among their residents (Howell et al., in press), yet few detention centers and juvenile correctional facilities screen admissions for gang involvement. The same can be said for the criminal justice system, with the exception of scant knowledge of prison gangs. Better screening and risk classification of offenders for gang involvement in juvenile and adult correctional facilities is imperative. This would help protect the public by giving correctional staff reliable information to classify gang offenders at the appropriate level of risk and to match juvenile offenders with gang treatment programs available in correctional facilities. Effective programs are needed in these facilities to prevent gang formation, membership, and victimization and to break up drug operations inside prisons.

◆ Programs are needed to break the cycle of gang members moving from communities to detention to corrections and prisons and back into communities (Howell and Decker, 1999). Ex-convicts need marketable job skills and gainful employment opportunities to avoid the lucrative drug market. Breaking this cycle becomes all the more important as States are imprisoning younger and younger offenders who now are returning to the streets at a younger age than in the past. Making effective drug treatment programs available, along with legitimate job opportunities, would also help break the cycle.

◆ Jurisdictions can control and reduce gang problems by targeting serious, violent, and chronic juvenile offenders who may not necessarily be known gang members. In jurisdictions that have gang problems, these offenders are very likely to be involved in them. Most gang members are known to the justice system and local social service agencies at some point in their gang careers. More effective intervention is needed, using risk and needs assessment technology, to better protect the public and improve rehabilitation efforts.

◆ Police should not be expected to assume sole responsibility for youth gang problems. Broad-based community collaboration is essential for long-term success. Communities that begin with suppression as their main response generally discover later that cooperation and collaboration between public and private community agencies and citizens are necessary for an effective solution. Considerable advantage accrues from involving the entire community from the outset, beginning with a comprehensive and systematic assessment of the presumed youth gang problem. Key community leaders must mobilize the resources of the entire community, guided by a consensus on definitions, program targets, and interrelated strategies. Comprehensive programs that incorporate prevention, intervention, and enforcement components are most likely to be effective.

◆ Preventing children and adolescents from joining gangs may be the most cost-effective solution, but little is known about how to do this. Providing alternatives for potential or current gang members appears to hold promise, particularly if gang conflicts are mediated at the same time. An antigang curriculum, especially if combined with afterschool or antibullying programs, may be effective. Because predictors for joining a gang and remaining in a gang span multiple domains—individual problems, family variables, school problems, peer group associations, and community conditions—programs that address multiple components appear to be the most effective.

Conclusion

Despite recent progress in preventing involvement in gangs during childhood and adolescence and in reducing serious and violent gang crime, the complexity of the youth gang problem defies an easy solution or single strategy. Current knowledge about which programs are effective in preventing and reducing youth gang problems is limited. The most effective program model will likely prove to be a combination of prevention, intervention, and suppression strategies integrated in a collaborative approach, supported by a management information system, and validated by rigorous evaluation. Communities across the country are undertaking collaborative efforts to deal with youth gangs, but few of these programs and strategies are being evaluated. State and local governments must undertake systematic examination of their youth gang programs and strategies. The knowledge gained about what is effective and what is not will benefit not only their own communities, but also communities across the Nation.

References

American Civil Liberties Union. 1997. *False Premise/ False Promise: The Blythe Street Gang Injunction.* Los Angeles, CA: ACLU Foundation of Southern California.

Aos, S., Phipps, P., Barnoski, R., and Lieb, R. 1999. *The Comparative Costs and Benefits of Programs To Reduce Crime: A Review of National Research Findings With Implications for Washington State.* Olympia, WA: Washington State Institute for Public Policy.

Arnette, J.L., and Walsleben, M.C. 1998. *Combating Fear and Restoring Safety in Schools.* Bulletin. Washington, DC: U.S. Department of Justice, Office of Justice Programs, Office of Juvenile Justice and Delinquency Prevention.

Atkinson, W.A. 1996. Organizing the community response in Aurora, Colorado. In *Gangs in America,* 2d ed., edited by C.R. Huff. Thousand Oaks, CA: Sage Publications, Inc., pp. 257–262.

Battin-Pearson, S.R., Guo, J., Hill, K.G., Abbott, R.D., and Hawkins, J.D. 1999. Early predictors of sustained adolescent gang membership. Unpublished manuscript. Seattle, WA: University of Washington, School of Social Work, Social Development Research Group.

Best, J., and Hutchinson, M.M. 1996. The gang initiation rite as a motif in contemporary crime discourse. *Justice Quarterly* 13:383–404.

Bjerregaard, B., and Smith, C. 1993. Gender differences in gang participation, delinquency, and substance use. *Journal of Quantitative Criminology* 9:329–355.

Block, R., and Block, C. 1993. *Street Gang Crime in Chicago.* Research in Brief. Washington, DC: U.S. Department of Justice, Office of Justice Programs, National Institute of Justice.

Block, R., and Jones, E. 1999. Identifying and describing core areas of gang activity using GIS. Paper presented at the annual meeting of the American Society of Criminology, Toronto, Canada, November.

Boys & Girls Clubs of Greater Fort Worth. 1996. *Comin' Up Gang Intervention Program Project Report.* Fort Worth, TX: Boys & Girls Clubs of Greater Fort Worth.

Brewer, D.D., Hawkins, J.D., Catalano, R.F., and Neckerman, H.J. 1995. Preventing serious, violent, and chronic juvenile offending. In *Sourcebook on Serious, Violent, and Chronic Juvenile Offenders,* edited by J.C. Howell, B. Krisberg, J.D. Hawkins, and J.J. Wilson. Thousand Oaks, CA: Sage Publications, Inc., pp. 61–141.

Burch, J.H., and Chemers, B.M. 1997. *A Comprehensive Response to America's Youth Gang Problem.* Fact Sheet #40. Washington, DC: U.S. Department of Justice, Office of Justice Programs, Office of Juvenile Justice and Delinquency Prevention.

Burch, J.H., and Kane, C.M. 1999. *Implementing the OJJDP Comprehensive Gang Model.* Fact Sheet #122. Washington, DC: U.S. Department of Justice, Office of Justice Programs, Office of Juvenile Justice and Delinquency Prevention.

Bureau of Justice Assistance. 1997a. *Addressing Community Gang Problems: A Model for Problem Solving.* Washington, DC: U.S. Department of Justice, Office of Justice Programs, Bureau of Justice Assistance.

Bureau of Justice Assistance. 1997b. *Urban Street Gang Enforcement*. Washington, DC: U.S. Department of Justice, Office of Justice Programs, Bureau of Justice Assistance.

Bureau of Justice Assistance. 1998. *Addressing Community Gang Problems: A Practical Guide*. Washington, DC: U.S. Department of Justice, Office of Justice Programs, Bureau of Justice Assistance.

Bursik, R.J., Jr., and Grasmick, H.G. 1993. *Neighborhoods and Crime: The Dimension of Effective Community Control*. New York, NY: Lexington Books.

Capizzi, M., Cook, J.I., and Schumacher, M. 1995. The TARGET model: A new approach to the prosecution of gang cases. *The Prosecutor* (Fall):18–21.

Caplan, N.S., Deshaies, D.J., Suttles, G.D., and Mattick, H.W. 1967. The nature, variety, and patterning of street club work in an urban setting. In *Juvenile Gangs in Context*, edited by M. Klein and B.G. Myerhoff. Englewood Cliffs, NJ: Prentice-Hall, pp. 194–202.

Carnegie Council on Adolescent Development. 1994. *A Matter of Time: Risk and Opportunity in the Nonschool Hours*. Abridged version. New York, NY: Carnegie Corporation of New York.

Center for Successful Child Development. 1993. Executive Summary in *Beethoven's Fifth: The First Five Years of the Center for Successful Child Development*. Chicago, IL: Ounce of Prevention Fund.

Chandler, K.A., Chapman, C.D., Rand, M.R., and Taylor, B.M. 1998. *Student Reports of School Crime: 1989 and 1995*. Washington, DC: U.S. Department of Justice, Office of Justice Programs, Bureau of Justice Statistics, and U.S. Department of Education, National Center for Education Statistics.

Chesney-Lind, M., Leisen, M.B., Allen, J., Brown, M., Rockhill, A., Marker, N., Liu, R., and Joe, K. 1995a. Crime, delinquency, and gangs in Hawaii: Evaluation of Hawaii's Youth Gang Response System: Part I. Unpublished report. Honolulu, HI: Center for Youth Research, Social Science Research Institute, University of Hawaii, Manoa.

Chesney-Lind, M., Leisen, M.B., Allen, J., Brown, M., Rockhill, A., Marker, N., Liu, R., and Joe, K. 1995b. The Youth Gang Response System. A process evaluation: Part II. Unpublished report. Honolulu, HI: Center for Youth Research, Social Science Research Institute, University of Hawaii, Manoa.

Chesney-Lind, M., Marker, N., Stern, I.R., Song, V., Reyes, H., Reyes, Y., Stern, J., Taira, J., and Yap, A. 1992. An evaluation of Act 189: Hawaii's response to youth gangs. Unpublished report. Honolulu, HI: Center for Youth Research, Social Science Research Institute, University of Hawaii, Manoa.

Chesney-Lind, M., Mayeda, D., Okamoto, S., Paramore, V., and Marker, N. 1999. Delinquency and gangs in Hawaii. Unpublished report. Honolulu, HI: Center for Youth Research, Social Science Research Institute, University of Hawaii, Manoa.

City of Fort Worth, TX. 1996. *Comin' Up Gang Intervention Program Background Information*. Press release. Forth Worth, TX: City of Forth Worth, TX.

Clark, J.R. 1997. LEN salutes its 1997 People of the Year, the Boston Gun Project Working Group. *Law Enforcement News* 23(1):4–5.

Cohen, M.I., Williams, K., Bekelman, A.M., and Crosse, S. 1994. Evaluation of the National Youth Gang Drug Prevention Program. Unpublished report to the Administration on Children, Youth and Families, U.S. Department of Health and Human Services.

Community Reclamation Project. 1990. *Rising Above Gangs and Drugs: How to Start a Community Reclamation Project*. Lomita, CA: Community Reclamation Project.

Conly, C.H. 1993. *Street Gangs: Current Knowledge and Statistics*. Washington, DC: U.S. Department of Justice, Office of Justice Programs, National Institute of Justice.

Corbet, R.P. 1998. The promise (and perils) of probation-police partnerships. *Corrections Management Quarterly* 2(Summer):3.

Corbet, R.P., Fitzgerald, B.L., and Jordan, J. 1996. Operation Night Light: An emerging model for police-probation partnerships. In *Invitation to Change: Better Government Competition on Public Safety*, edited by L. Brown and K. Ciffolillo. Boston, MA: Pioneer Institute for Public Policy Research.

Cotton, P. 1992. Violence decreases with gang truce. *The Journal of the American Medical Association* 268:443–444.

Cronin, R. 1994. *Innovative Community Partnerships: Working Together for Change*. Program Summary. Washington, DC: U.S. Department of Justice, Office of Justice Programs, Office of Juvenile Justice and Delinquency Prevention.

Curry, G.D. 1995. Gang community, gang involvement, gang crime. Unpublished paper presented at the annual meeting of the American Sociological Association, Washington, DC, August.

Curry, G.D. 1998. Female gang involvement. *Journal of Research on Crime and Delinquency* 35(1):100–118.

Curry, G.D. In press. Self-reported gang involvement and officially recorded delinquency. *Criminology.*

Curry, G.D., and Decker, S.H. 1998. *Confronting Gangs: Crime and Community*. Los Angeles, CA: Roxbury Publishing Company.

Curry, G.D., Williams, K., and Koenemann, L. 1997. Race and ethnic differences in female gang involvement. Unpublished paper presented at the annual meeting of the Academy of Criminal Justice Sciences, Lexington, KY, March.

Dahmann, J. 1981. *Operation Hardcore, A Prosecutorial Response to Violent Gang Criminality: Interim Evaluation Report*. Washington, DC: Mitre Corporation. Reprinted in *The Modern Gang Reader*, edited by M.A. Klein, C.L. Maxson, and J. Miller, 1995. Los Angeles, CA: Roxbury Publishing Company, pp. 301–303.

Decker, S.H. 1996. Collective and normative features of gang violence. *Justice Quarterly* 13:243–264.

Decker, S.H., Bynum, T.S., and Weisel, D.L. 1998. Gangs as organized crime groups: A tale of two cities. *Justice Quarterly* 15:395–423.

Decker, S.H., and Van Winkle, B. 1996. *Life in the Gang: Family, Friends, and Violence*. New York, NY: Cambridge University Press.

Deschenes, E.P., and Esbensen, F. 1999. Violence in gangs: Gender differences in perceptions and behavior. *Journal of Quantitative Criminology* 15(1):53–96.

DiIulio, J., Jr. 1996. They're coming: Florida's youth crime bomb. *Impact* (Spring):25–27.

Duxbury, E.B. 1993. Correctional interventions. In *The Gang Intervention Handbook*, edited by A.P. Goldstein and C.R. Huff. Champaign, IL: Research Press, pp. 427–437.

Eisenhower Foundation. 1990. *Youth Investment and Community Reconstruction: Street Lessons on Drugs and Crime for the Nineties*. Washington, DC: Eisenhower Foundation.

Esbensen, F., and Deschenes, E.P. 1998. A multisite examination of youth gang membership: Does gender matter? *Criminology* 36:799–827.

Esbensen, F., Deschenes, E.P., and Winfree, L.T. 1999. Differences between gang girls and gang boys: Results from a multi-site survey. *Youth and Society* 31(1):27–53.

Esbensen, F., Huizinga, D., and Weiher, A.W. 1993. Gang and non-gang youth: Differences in explanatory variables. *Journal of Contemporary Criminal Justice* 9(1):94–116.

Esbensen, F., and Osgood, D.W. 1997. *National Evaluation of G.R.E.A.T.* Research in Brief. Washington, DC: U.S. Department of Justice, Office of Justice Programs, National Institute of Justice.

Esbensen, F., and Osgood, D.W. 1999. Gang Resistance Education and Training (GREAT): Results from the national evaluation. *Journal of Research in Crime and Delinquency* 36(2):194–225.

Esbensen, F., and Winfree, L.T. 1998. Race and gender differences between gang and non-gang youth: Results from a multi-site survey. *Justice Quarterly* 15(3):505–526.

Feyerherm, W., Pope, C., and Lovell, R. 1992. Youth gang prevention and early intervention programs. Final research report. Unpublished manuscript. Portland, OR: Portland State University.

Finn, P., and Healey, K.M. 1996. *Preventing Gang- and Drug-Related Witness Intimidation.* Washington, DC: U.S. Department of Justice, Office of Justice Programs, National Institute of Justice.

Fleisher, M.S. 1995. *Beggars and Thieves: Lives of Urban Street Criminals.* Madison, WI: University of Wisconsin Press.

Fleisher, M.S. 1998. *Dead End Kids: Gang Girls and the Boys They Know.* Madison, WI: University of Wisconsin.

Fritsch, E.J., Caeti, T.J., and Taylor, R.W. 1999. Gang suppression through saturation patrol, aggressive curfew, and truancy enforcement: A quasi-experimental test of the Dallas anti-gang initiative. *Crime and Delinquency* 45:122–139.

Gaouette, N. 1997. Hope rises at Homeboy Bakeries in L.A. *Christian Science Monitor* (September 15):1.

Gates, J. 1998. (November 17). Inner-City Games and Knowledge Adventure Software team up to help inner-city youths exercise mind and body. News release. Torrance, CA: Knowledge Adventure, Inc.

Geis, G. 1965. *Juvenile Gangs.* Report to the President's Committee on Youth Crime. Washington, DC: U.S. Government Printing Office.

Genelin, M. 1993. Gang prosecution: The hardest game in town. In *The Gang Intervention Handbook,* edited by A.P. Goldstein and C.R. Huff. Champaign, IL: Research Press, pp. 417–426.

Gold, M., and Mattick, H. 1974. *Experiment in the Streets: the Chicago Youth Development Project.* Ann Arbor, MI: Institute for Social Research, University of Michigan.

Goldstein, A.P. 1993. Interpersonal skills training interventions. In *The Gang Intervention Handbook,* edited by A.P. Goldstein and C.R. Huff. Champaign, IL: Research Press, pp. 87–157.

Goldstein, A.P., and Glick, B. 1994. *The Prosocial Gang: Implementing Aggression Replacement Training.* Thousand Oaks, CA: Sage Publications, Inc.

Goldstein, A.P., Glick, B., and Gibbs, J.C. 1998. *Aggression Replacement Training: A Comprehensive Intervention for Aggressive Youth.* Champaign, IL: Research Press.

Goldstein, A.P., and Huff, C.R., eds. 1993. *The Gang Intervention Handbook.* Champaign, IL: Research Press.

Goldstein, A.P., and Kodluboy, D.W. 1998. *Gangs in Schools: Signs, Symbols, and Solutions.* Champaign, IL: Research Press.

Goldstein, H. 1979. Improving policing: A problem-oriented approach. *Crime and Delinquency* 25(2): 236–258.

Goldstein, H. 1990. *Problem-Oriented Policing.* New York, NY: McGraw Hill.

Gottfredson, G.D., and Gottfredson, D.C. 1996. A National Study of Delinquency Prevention in Schools: Rationale for a study to describe the extensiveness and implementation of programs to prevent problem behavior in schools. Unpublished report. Ellicott City, MD: Gottfredson Associates.

Gottfredson, G.D., and Gottfredson, D.C. 1999. Survey of School-Based Gang Prevention and Intervention Programs: Preliminary findings. Paper presented at the National Youth Gang Symposium, Las Vegas, NV, July 29.

Groves, B.M., Zuckerman, B., Marans, S., and Cohen, D.J. 1993. Silent victims: Children who witness violence. *Journal of the American Medical Association* 269:262–264.

Hagedorn, J M. 1988. *People and Folks: Gangs, Crime, and the Underclass in a Rustbelt City.* Chicago, IL: Lakeview Press.

Hagedorn, J.M. 1998. Gang violence in the post-industrial era. In *Youth Violence,* edited by M. Tonry and M. Moore, Crime and Justice Series, vol. 24. Chicago, IL: University of Chicago Press, pp. 365–420.

Hawkins, J.D., Herrenkohl, T., Farrington, D.P., Brewer, D., Catalano, R.F., and Harachi, T.W. 1998. A review of predictors of violence. In *Serious and Violent Juvenile Offenders: Risk Factors and Successful Interventions*, edited by R. Loeber and D.P. Farrington. Thousand Oaks, CA: Sage Publications, Inc.

Hemmens, C. and Bennett, K. 1999. Juvenile curfews and the courts: Judicial response to a not-so-new crime control strategy. *Crime and Delinquency* 45:99–121.

Henggeler, S.W. 1997. *Treating Serious Anti-Social Behavior in Youth: The MST Approach*. Bulletin. Washington, DC: U.S. Department of Justice, Office of Justice Programs, Office of Juvenile Justice and Delinquency Prevention.

Hill, K.G., Howell, J.C., Hawkins, J.D., and Battin-Pearson, S.R. 1999. Childhood risk factors for adolescent gang membership: Results from the Seattle Social Development Project. *Journal of Research in Crime and Delinquency* 36(3):300–322.

Hoffman, P., and Silverstein, M. 1995. Safe streets don't require lifting rights. In *The Modern Gang Reader*, edited by M.W. Klein, C.L. Maxson, and J. Miller. Los Angeles, CA: Roxbury, p. 333.

Houston, J. 1996. What works: The search for excellence in gang intervention programs. *The Journal of Gang Research* 3:1–16.

Howell, J.C., ed. 1995. *Guide for Implementing the Comprehensive Strategy for Serious, Violent, and Chronic Juvenile Offenders*. Washington, DC: U.S. Department of Justice, Office of Justice Programs, Office of Juvenile Justice and Delinquency Prevention.

Howell, J.C. 1998a. Promising programs for youth gang violence prevention and intervention. In *Serious and Violent Juvenile Offenders: Risk Factors and Successful Interventions*, edited by R. Loeber and D.P. Farrington. Thousand Oaks, CA: Sage Publications, Inc., pp. 284–312.

Howell, J.C. 1998b. *Youth Gangs: An Overview*. Bulletin. Washington, DC: U.S. Department of Justice, Office of Justice Programs, Office of Juvenile Justice and Delinquency Prevention.

Howell, J.C. 1999. Youth gang homicides: A literature review. *Crime and Delinquency* 45(2):208–241.

Howell, J.C. 2000. Youth gangs have changed. Paper presented at the 27th National Conference on Juvenile Justice. Tampa, FL, March 20.

Howell, J.C., Curry, G.D., Roush, D., and Pontius, M. In press. National Survey of Gang Problems in Juvenile Detention Facilities. Unpublished final report. Richmond, KY: National Juvenile Detention Association.

Howell, J.C., and Decker, S.H. 1999. *The Youth Gangs, Drugs, and Violence Connection*. Bulletin. Washington, DC: U.S. Department of Justice, Office of Justice Programs, Office of Juvenile Justice and Delinquency Prevention.

Howell, J.C., and Gleason, D.K. 1999. *Youth Gang Drug Trafficking*. Bulletin. Washington, DC: U.S. Department of Justice, Office of Justice Programs, Office of Juvenile Justice and Delinquency Prevention.

Howell, J.C., and Hawkins, J.D. 1998. Prevention of youth violence. In *Youth Violence*, edited by M. Tonry and M. Moore, Crime and Justice Series, vol. 24. Chicago, IL: University of Chicago Press, pp. 263–315.

Howell, J.C., and Lynch, J.P. In press. *Youth Gangs in Schools*. Bulletin. Washington, DC: U.S. Department of Justice, Office of Justice Programs, Office of Juvenile Justice and Delinquency Prevention.

Huff, C.R. 1989. Youth gangs and public policy. *Crime and Delinquency* 35:524–537.

Huff, C.R. 1996. The criminal behavior of gang members and non-gang at-risk youth. In *Gangs in America*, 2d ed., edited by C.R. Huff. Thousand Oaks, CA: Sage Publications, Inc., pp. 75–102.

Huff, C.R. 1998. *Comparing the Criminal Behavior of Youth Gangs and At-Risk Youth*. Research in Brief. Washington, DC: U.S. Department of Justice, Office of Justice Programs, National Institute of Justice.

Hunt, A.L., and Weiner, K. 1977. The impact of a juvenile curfew: Suppression and displacement patterns of juvenile offenses. *Journal of Police Science and Administration* 5(4):407–412.

Hunzeker, D. 1993. Ganging up against violence. *State Legislatures*. Denver, CO: National Conference of State Legislatures, pp. 28–31.

Hutson, H.R., Anglin, D., Kyriacou, N., Hart, J., and Spears, K. 1995. The epidemic of gang-related homicides in Los Angeles County from 1979 through 1994. *Journal of the American Medical Association* 274:1031–1036.

Hutson, H.R., Anglin, D., and Pratts, M.J. 1994. Adolescents and children injured or killed in drive-by shootings in Los Angeles. *New England Journal of Medicine* 330(5):324–327.

Illinois Criminal Justice Information Authority. 1999. Reducing youth gang violence in urban areas: One community's effort. *On Good Authority* 2(5):1–4.

Jackson, R.K., and McBride, W.D. 1985. *Understanding Street Gangs*. Plackerville, CA: Custom Publishing.

Johnson, C., Webster, B., and Connors, E. 1995. *Prosecuting Gangs: A National Assessment*. Research in Brief. Washington, DC: U.S. Department of Justice, Office of Justice Programs, National Institute of Justice.

Josi, D., and Sechrest, D.K. 1999. A pragmatic approach to parole aftercare: Evaluation of a community reintegration program for high-risk youthful offenders. *Justice Quarterly* 16(1):51–80.

Kelling, G.L., Hochberg, R.R., Kaminska, S.L., Rocheleau, A.M., Rosenbaum, D.P., Roth, J.A., and Skogan, W.G. 1998. *The Bureau of Justice Assistance Comprehensive Communities Program: A Preliminary Report*. Research in Brief. Washington, DC: U.S. Department of Justice, Office of Justice Programs, National Institute of Justice.

Kennedy, D.M. 1997. Pulling levers: Chronic offenders, high-crime settings, and a theory of prevention. *Valparaiso University Law Review* 31:449–483.

Kennedy, D.M., Piehl, A M., and Braga, A.A. 1996. Youth violence in Boston: Gun markets, serious youth offenders, and a use-reduction strategy. *Law and Contemporary Problems* 59:147–196. Special Issue.

Kent, D.R., Donaldson, S.I., Wyrick, P.A., and Smith, P.J. 2000. Evaluating criminal justice programs designed to reduce gang crime by targeting repeat gang offenders. *Evaluation and Program Planning* 23(1):115–124.

Kent, D.R., and Smith, P. 1995. The Tri-Agency Resource Gang Enforcement Team: A selective approach to reduce gang crime. In *The Modern Gang Reader*, edited by M.W. Klein, C.L. Maxson, and J. Miller. Los Angeles, CA: Roxbury, pp. 292–296.

Klein, M.W. 1968. The Ladino Hills project: Final report. Unpublished. Los Angeles, CA: University of Southern California, Youth Studies Center.

Klein, M.W. 1969. Gang cohesiveness, delinquency, and a street-work program. *Journal of Research in Crime and Delinquency* 6(2):135–166.

Klein, M.W. 1971. *Street Gangs and Street Workers*. Englewood Cliffs, NJ: Prentice-Hall.

Klein, M.W. 1995a. *The American Street Gang*. New York, NY: Oxford University Press.

Klein, M.W. 1995b. Street gang cycles. In *Crime*, edited by J.Q. Wilson and J. Petersilia. San Francisco, CA: Institute for Contemporary Studies, pp. 217–236.

Klein, M.W., Maxson, C.L., and Miller, J., eds. 1995. *The Modern Gang Reader*. Los Angeles, CA: Roxbury Publishing Company.

Kobrin, S. 1959. The Chicago Area Project: A twenty-five year assessment. *Annals of the American Academy of Political and Social Science* 322:19–29.

Kodluboy, D.W., and Evenrud, L.A. 1993. School-based interventions: Best practices and critical issues. In *The Gang Intervention Handbook*, edited by A. Goldstein and C.R. Huff. Champaign, IL: Research Press, pp. 257–299.

Kracke, K. 1996. *SafeFutures: Partnerships To Reduce Youth Violence and Delinquency*. Fact Sheet #38. Washington, DC: U.S. Department of Justice, Office of Justice Programs, Office of Juvenile Justice and Delinquency Prevention.

Lally, J.R., Mangione, P.L., and Honig, A.S. 1988. The Syracuse University Family Development Research Project: Long-range impact of an early intervention with low-income children and their families. In *Annual Advances in Applied Developmental Psychology,* vol. 3, edited by R. Powell. Norwood, NJ: Ablex, pp. 79–104.

Lasley, J. 1998. *"Designing Out" Gang Homicides and Street Assaults.* Research in Brief. Washington, DC: U.S. Department of Justice, Office of Justice Programs, National Institute of Justice.

LeBoeuf, D. 1996. *Curfew: An Answer to Juvenile Delinquency and Victimization?* Bulletin. Washington, DC: U.S. Department of Justice, Office of Justice Programs, Office of Juvenile Justice and Delinquency Prevention.

Lesce, T. 1993. Gang resistance education and training (G.R.E.A.T.). *Law and Order* 41:47–50.

Lindsay, B., and McGillis, D. 1986. Citywide community crime prevention: An assessment of the Seattle program. In *Community Crime Prevention: Does It Work?,* edited by D.P. Rosenbaum. Beverly Hills, CA: Sage Publications, Inc., pp. 46–67.

Lipsey, M.W., and Wilson, D.B. 1998. Effective interventions with serious juvenile offenders: A synthesis of research. In *Serious and Violent Juvenile Offenders: Risk Factors and Successful Interventions,* edited by R. Loeber and D.P. Farrington. Thousand Oaks, CA: Sage Publications, Inc.

Loeber, R., and Farrington, D.P., eds. 1997. *Never Too Early, Never Too Late: Risk Factors and Successful Interventions for Serious and Violent Juvenile Offenders.* Final Report of the Study Group on Serious and Violent Juvenile Offenders (grant number 95–JD–FX–0018). Washington, DC: U.S. Department of Justice, Office of Justice Programs, Office of Juvenile Justice and Delinquency Prevention.

Loeber, R., and Farrington, D.P., eds. 1998. *Serious and Violent Juvenile Offenders: Risk Factors and Successful Interventions.* Thousand Oaks, CA: Sage Publications, Inc.

Los Angeles City Attorney Gang Prosecution Section. 1995. Civil gang abatement: A community based policing tool of the Office of the Los Angeles City Attorney. In *The Modern Gang Reader,* edited by M.W. Klein, C.L. Maxson, and J. Miller. Los Angeles, CA: Roxbury, pp. 325–331.

Marans, S., and Berkman, M. 1997. *Child Development-Community Policing: Partnership in a Climate of Violence.* Bulletin. Washington, DC: U.S. Department of Justice, Office of Justice Programs, Office of Juvenile Justice and Delinquency Prevention.

Mattick, H., and Caplan, N.S. 1962. *Chicago Youth Development Project: The Chicago Boys Club.* Ann Arbor, MI: Institute for Social Research.

Maxson, C.L., Whitlock, M.L., and Klein, M.W. 1998. Vulnerability to street gang membership: Implications for prevention. *Social Service Review* (March):70–91.

Maxson, C.L., Woods, K., and Klein, M.W. 1995. Street gang migration: How big a threat? *National Institute of Justice Journal* 230:26–31.

McBride, W.D. 1993. Police departments and gang intervention: The Operation Safe Streets concept. In *The Gang Intervention Handbook,* edited by A. Goldstein and C.R. Huff. Champaign, IL: Research Press, pp. 411–415.

Medaris, M.L., Campbell, E., and James, B. 1997. *Sharing Information: A Guide to the Family Educational Rights and Privacy Act and Participation in Juvenile Justice Programs.* Washington, DC: U.S. Department of Justice, Office of Justice Programs, Office of Juvenile Justice and Delinquency Prevention.

Melton, G.B., Limber, S.P., Cunningham, P., Osgood, D.W., Chambers, J., Flerx, V., Henggeler, S., and Nation, M. 1998. *Violence Among Rural Youth.* Final report to the Office of Juvenile Justice and Delinquency Prevention. Washington, DC: U.S. Department of Justice, Office of Justice Programs, Office of Juvenile Justice and Delinquency Prevention.

Miethe, T.D., and McCorkle, R.C. 1997a. Evaluating Nevada's anti-gang legislation and gang prosecution units. Unpublished report. Washington, DC: U.S. Department of Justice, Office of Justice Programs, National Institute of Justice.

Miethe, T.D., and McCorkle, R.C. 1997b. Gang membership and criminal processing: A test of the "master status" concept. *Justice Quarterly* 14(3):407–427.

Miller, W.B. 1962. The impact of a "total community" delinquency control project. *Social Problems* 10:168–191.

Miller, W.B. 1990. Why the United States has failed to solve its youth gang problem. In *Gangs in America*, edited by C.R. Huff. Newbury Park, CA: Sage Publications, Inc., pp. 263–287.

Miller, W.B. 1992 (Revised from 1982). *Crime by Youth Gangs and Groups in the United States*. Washington, DC: U.S. Department of Justice, Office of Justice Programs, Office of Juvenile Justice and Delinquency Prevention.

Miller, W.B. In press. *The Growth of Youth Gang Problems in the United States: 1970–1995*. Washington, DC: U.S. Department of Justice, Office of Justice Programs, Office of Juvenile Justice and Delinquency Prevention.

Moore, J.P. 1997. *Highlights of the 1995 Youth Gang Survey*. Fact Sheet #63. Washington, DC: U.S. Department of Justice, Office of Justice Programs, Office of Juvenile Justice and Delinquency Prevention.

Moore, J.P., and Cook, I.L. 1999. *Highlights of the 1998 National Youth Gang Survey*. Fact Sheet #123. Washington, DC: U.S. Department of Justice, Office of Justice Programs, Office of Juvenile Justice and Delinquency Prevention.

Moore, J.P., and Terrett, C. 1998. *Highlights of the 1996 National Youth Gang Survey*. Fact Sheet #86. Washington, DC: U.S. Department of Justice, Office of Justice Programs, Office of Juvenile Justice and Delinquency Prevention.

Moore, J.W. 1978. *Homeboys: Gangs, Drugs and Prison in the Barrios of Los Angeles*. Philadelphia, PA: Temple University Press.

Moore, J.W. 1991. *Going Down to the Barrio: Homeboys and Homegirls in Change*. Philadelphia, PA: Temple University Press.

Moore, J.W., and Vigil, J.D. 1993. Barrios in transition. In *In the Barrios: Latinos and the Underclass Debate*, edited by J.W. Moore and R. Pinderhughes. New York, NY: Russell Sage Foundation, pp. 27–49.

National Center for Neighborhood Enterprise. 1999. *Violence-Free Zone Initiatives: Models of Successful Grassroots Youth Intervention*. Washington, DC: National Center for Neighborhood Enterprise.

National Crime Prevention Council. 1996. *New Ways of Working with Local Laws to Reduce Crime*. Washington, DC: National Crime Prevention Council.

National Criminal Justice Association. 1997. *Juvenile Justice Reform Initiatives in the States, 1994–1996*. Washington, DC: U.S. Department of Justice, Office of Justice Programs, Office of Juvenile Justice and Delinquency Prevention.

National Drug Intelligence Center. 1994. *NDIC Street Gang Symposium*. Pub. No. 94–M0119–002. Washington, DC: National Drug Intelligence Center.

National Drug Intelligence Center. 1995. *NDIC Street Gang Symposium: Selected Findings*. Pub. No. 94–M0119–002A. Washington, DC: National Drug Intelligence Center.

National Youth Gang Center. 1997. *1995 National Youth Gang Survey*. Program Summary. Washington, DC: U.S. Department of Justice, Office of Justice Programs, Office of Juvenile Justice and Delinquency Prevention.

National Youth Gang Center. 1999. *1996 National Youth Gang Survey*. Summary. Washington, DC: U.S. Department of Justice, Office of Justice Programs, Office of Juvenile Justice and Delinquency Prevention.

National Youth Gang Center. In press. *1998 National Youth Gang Survey*. Summary. Washington, DC: U.S. Department of Justice, Office of Justice Programs, Office of Juvenile Justice and Delinquency Prevention.

Needle, J., and Stapleton, W.V. 1983. *Police Handling of Youth Gangs*. Washington, DC: U.S. Department of Justice, Office of Justice Programs, Office of Juvenile Justice and Delinquency Prevention.

New York City Youth Board. 1960. *Reaching the Fighting Gang*. New York, NY: New York City Youth Board.

Office of the Attorney General. 1995. *Anti-Violent Crime Initiative: The First Year (March 1994–February 1995)*. Report to the President. Washington, DC: U.S. Department of Justice.

Office for Victims of Crime. 1996. *Victims of Violence: A New Frontier in Victim Services*. Washington, DC: U.S. Department of Justice, Office of Justice Programs, Office for Victims of Crime.

Office of Juvenile Justice and Delinquency Prevention. 1995a. *Delinquency Prevention Works*. Program Summary. Washington, DC: U.S. Department of Justice, Office of Justice Programs, Office of Juvenile Justice and Delinquency Prevention.

Office of Juvenile Justice and Delinquency Prevention. 1995b. *Matrix of Community-Based Initiatives*. Program Summary. Washington, DC: U.S. Department of Justice, Office of Justice Programs, Office of Juvenile Justice and Delinquency Prevention.

Office of Juvenile Justice and Delinquency Prevention. 1999. *Promising Strategies To Reduce Gun Violence*. Report. Washington, DC: U.S. Department of Justice, Office of Justice Programs, Office of Juvenile Justice and Delinquency Prevention.

Olweus, D. 1991. Bully/victim problems among schoolchildren: Basic facts and effects of a school based intervention. In *The Development and Treatment of Childhood Aggression*, edited by D.J. Pepler and K.H. Rubin. Hillsdale, NJ: Erlbaum.

Olweus, D. 1992. Bullying among school children: Intervention and prevention. In *Aggression and Violence Throughout the Life Span*, edited by R.D. Peters, R.J. McMahon, and V.L. Qinsey. Newbury Park, CA: Sage Publications, Inc., pp. 100–125.

Orange County Chiefs' and Sheriff's Association. 1999. *The Final Report of the Orange County Consortium COPS Project*. Westminster, CA: Orange County Chiefs' and Sheriff's Association County-Wide Gang Strategy Steering Committee.

Palumbo, D.J., and Ferguson, J.L. 1995. Evaluating Gang Resistance Education and Training (GREAT): Is the impact the same as that of Drug Abuse Resistance Education (DARE)? *Evaluation Review* 19(6):597–619.

Parks and Community Services Department. 1997. Comin' Up Gang Intervention Program: Evaluation of major components. Unpublished. Fort Worth, TX: Parks and Community Services Department, City of Fort Worth.

Parsons, K.J.B., and Meeker, J.W. 1999. The connection between gangs and drugs: Drug-related analysis from the Gang Incident Tracking System. Paper presented at the annual meeting of the American Society of Criminology, Toronto, November.

Pennell, S. 1983. *San Diego Street Youth Program: Final Evaluation*. San Diego, CA: Association of Governments.

Powell, K.E., and Hawkins D.F., eds. 1996 (September/October). Youth violence prevention: Descriptions and baseline data from 13 evaluation projects. *American Journal of Preventive Medicine*. Supplement to vol. 12.

Pratcher, S.D. 1994 (December). A response to juvenile curfew violations. *Police Chief* 61:58.

Pyle, A. 1995. County takes first step to prohibiting gangs from parks. In *The Modern Gang Reader*, edited by M.W. Klein, C.L. Maxson, and J. Miller. Los Angeles, CA: Roxbury, p. 332.

Pynoos, R.S., and Nader, K. 1988. Psychological first aid and treatment approach to children exposed to community violence: Research implications. *Journal of Traumatic Stress* 1:445–473.

Rackauckas, T. 1999. *1998 Annual Report, Gang Unit and Tri-Agency Resource, Gang Enforcement Teams (TARGET)*. Santa Ana, CA: Orange County District Attorney's Office.

Ralph, P., Hunter, R.J., Marquart, J.W., Cuvelier, S.J., Merianos, D. 1996. Exploring the differences between gang and non-gang prisoners. In *Gangs in America*, 2d ed., edited by C.R. Huff. Thousand Oaks, CA: Sage Publications, Inc., pp. 241–256.

Ribisl, K.M., and Davidson, W.S. II. 1993. Community change interventions. In *The Gang Intervention Handbook*, edited by A. Goldstein and C.R. Huff. Champaign, IL: Research Press, pp. 333–355.

Rich, T. 1999. Mapping the path to problem solving. *National Institute of Justice Journal* October:2–9.

Rosenbaum, D.P., Lewis, D.A., and Grant, J.A. 1986. Neighborhood-based crime prevention: Assessing the efficacy of community organizing in Chicago. In *Community Crime Prevention: Does It Work?*, edited by D.P. Rosenbaum. Beverly Hills, CA: Sage Publications, Inc., pp. 109–133.

Rosenfeld, R., and Decker, S.H. 1996. Consent to search and seize: Evaluating an innovative youth firearm suppression program. *Law and Contemporary Problems* 59(Special Issue):197–220.

Ruefle, W., and Reynolds, K M. 1995. Curfew and delinquency in major American cities. *Crime and Delinquency* 41:347–363.

Rutter, M., Giller, H., and Hagell, A. 1998. *Antisocial Behavior by Young People*. New York, NY: Cambridge University Press.

Sanders, W. 1994. *Gangbangs and Drive-Bys: Grounded Culture and Juvenile Gang Violence*. New York, NY: Aldin de Gruyter.

Schlossman, S., and Sedlak, M. 1983. The Chicago Area Project revisited. *Crime and Delinquency* 29: 398–462.

Schumacher, M., and Kurz, G. 2000. *The 8% Solution: Preventing Serious, Repeat Juvenile Crime*. Thousand Oaks, CA: Sage Publications, Inc.

Schweinhart, L.J., Barnes, H.V., and Weikart, D.P. 1993. *Significant Benefits: The High/Scope Perry Preschool Study Through Age 27*. Ypsilanti, MI: High/Scope Press.

Shaw, C.R. 1930. *The Jack Roller: A Delinquent Boy's Own Story*. Chicago, IL: University of Chicago.

Shaw, C.R., and McKay, H.D. 1931. *Social Factors in Juvenile Delinquency. Report on the Causes of Crime*, vol. 11, National Commission on Law Observance and Enforcement. Washington, DC: U.S. Government Printing Office.

Shepherd, R.E. 1996. The proliferation of juvenile curfews. *American Bar Association Criminal Justice Section Newsletter* (September):1–3.

Sherman, L.W. 1990 (March–April). Police crackdowns: Initial and residual deterrence. In *Crime and Justice: A Review of Research*, vol. 12, edited by M. Tonry and N. Morris. Chicago, IL: University of Chicago, pp. 1–48.

Short, J.F., Jr. 1963. Street corner groups and patterns of delinquency: A progress report. *American Catholic Sociological Review* 28:13–32.

Short, J.F., Jr. 1996. Personal, gang, and community careers. In *Gangs in America*, 2d ed., edited by C.R. Huff. Thousand Oaks, CA: Sage Publications, Inc., pp. 221–240.

Short, J.F., Jr., and Strodtbeck, F.L. 1965. *Group Process and Gang Delinquency*. Chicago, IL: University of Chicago.

Skolnick, J.H., Correl, T., Navarro, E., and Rabb, R. 1988. The social structure of street drug dealing. Unpublished report to the Office of the Attorney General of the State of California, University of California, Berkeley.

Smith, C.S., Farrant, M.R., and Marchant, H.J. 1972. *The Wincroft Youth Project*. London, England: Tavistock Publications.

Smith, P.K., and Sharp, S. 1994. *School Bullying*. London, England: Routledge.

Snyder, H.N., and Sickmund, M. 1999. *Juvenile Offenders and Victims: 1999 National Report*. Washington, DC: U.S. Department of Justice, Office of Justice Programs, Office of Juvenile Justice and Delinquency Prevention.

Sorrentino, A. 1959. The Chicago Area Project after twenty-five years. *Federal Probation* 23:40–45.

Sorrentino, A., and Whittaker, D.W. 1994. The Chicago Area Project: Addressing the gang problem. *FBI Law Enforcement Bulletin* (May):7–12.

Spergel, I.A. 1966. *Street Gang Work: Theory and Practice.* Reading, MA: Addison-Wesley.

Spergel, I.A. 1972. Community action research as a political process. In *Community Organization: Studies in Constraint,* edited by I.A. Spergel. Beverly Hills, CA: Sage Publications, Inc., pp. 231–262.

Spergel, I.A. 1986. The violent youth gang in Chicago: A local community approach. *Social Service Review* 60:94–131.

Spergel, I.A. 1991. Youth gangs: Problem and response. Unpublished report to the U.S. Department of Justice, Office of Justice Programs, Office of Juvenile Justice and Delinquency Prevention.

Spergel, I.A. 1995. *The Youth Gang Problem.* New York, NY: Oxford University Press.

Spergel, I.A. 1999. Social intervention: The community youth worker (outreach) approach. Unpublished manuscript. Chicago, IL: University of Chicago, School of Social Service Administration.

Spergel, I.A., Chance, R.L., Ehrensaft, K., Regulus, T., Kane, C., and Alexander, A. 1992a. Prototype/models for gang intervention and suppression. Unpublished report to the U.S. Department of Justice, Office of Justice Programs, Office of Juvenile Justice and Delinquency Prevention.

Spergel, I.A., Chance, R.L., Ehrensaft, K., Regulus, T., Kane, C., and Laseter, R. 1992b. Technical assistance manuals: National youth gang suppression and intervention program. Unpublished report to the U.S. Department of Justice, Office of Justice Programs, Office of Juvenile Justice and Delinquency Prevention.

Spergel, I.A., Chance, R., Ehrensaft, K., Regulus, T., Kane, C., Laseter, R., Alexander, A., and Oh, S. 1994. *Gang Suppression and Intervention: Community Models.* Washington, DC: U.S. Department of Justice, Office of Justice Programs, Office of Juvenile Justice and Delinquency Prevention.

Spergel, I.A., and Curry, G.D. 1990. Strategies and perceived agency effectiveness in dealing with the youth gang problem. In *Gangs in America,* edited by C.R. Huff. Newbury Park, CA: Sage Publications, Inc., pp. 288–309.

Spergel, I.A., and Curry, G.D. 1993. The national youth gang survey: A research and development process. In *The Gang Intervention Handbook,* edited by A. Goldstein and C.R. Huff. Champaign, IL: Research Press, pp. 359–400.

Spergel, I.A., Curry, G.D., Chance, R., Kane, C., Ross, R., Alexander, A., Simmons, E., and Oh, S. 1994. *Gang Suppression and Intervention: Problem and Response.* Washington, DC: U.S. Department of Justice, Office of Justice Programs, Office of Juvenile Justice and Delinquency Prevention.

Spergel, I.A., and Grossman, S.F. 1997. The Little Village Project: A community approach to the gang problem. *Social Work* 42:456–470.

Spergel, I.A., Grossman, S.F., and Wa, K.M. 1998. The Little Village Gang Violence Reduction Program: A three year evaluation. Unpublished report. Chicago, IL: University of Chicago, School of Social Service Administration.

Spergel, I.A., Turner, C., Pleas, J., and Brown, P. 1969. Youth manpower: What happened in Woodlawn. Unpublished manuscript. Chicago, IL: University of Chicago, School of Social Service Administration.

Takata, S.R., and Tyler, C. 1994. A community-university based approach to gang intervention: Racine's innovative model for small cities. *Journal of Gang Research* 2:25–38.

Thomas, C.R. 1996. The Second Chance program. Unpublished paper presented at the National Youth Gang Symposium, Dallas, TX, June.

Thompson, D.W., and Jason, L.A. 1988. Street gangs and preventive interventions. *Criminal Justice Behavior* 15:323–333.

Thornberry, T.P. 1998. Membership in youth gangs and involvement in serious and violent offending. In *Serious and Violent Juvenile Offenders*, edited by R. Loeber and D.P. Farrington. Thousand Oaks, CA: Sage Publications, Inc., pp. 147–166.

Thornberry, T.P., and Burch, J.H. 1997. *Gang Members and Delinquent Behav*ior. Bulletin. Washington, DC: U.S. Department of Justice, Office of Justice Programs, Office of Juvenile Justice and Delinquency Prevention.

Thornberry, T.P., Huizinga, D., and Loeber, R. 1995. The prevention of serious delinquency and violence: Implications from the Program of Research on the Causes and Correlates of Delinquency. In *A Sourcebook: Serious, Violent, and Chronic Juvenile Offenders*, edited by J.C. Howell, B. Krisberg, J.D. Hawkins, and J.J. Wilson. Thousand Oaks, CA: Sage Publications, Inc., pp. 213–237.

Thrasher, F.M. 1927. *The Gang: A Study of 1,313 Gangs in Chicago*. Chicago, IL: University of Chicago.

Thrasher, F.M. 1936. The boys' club and juvenile delinquency. *American Journal of Sociology* 41:66–80.

Thurman, Q.C., Giacomazzi, A.L., Reisig, M.D., and Mueller, D.G. 1996. Community-based gang prevention and intervention: An evaluation of the Neutral Zone. *Crime and Delinquency* 42:279–295.

Torres, D.M. 1981. *Gang Violence Reduction Project 3rd Evaluation Report*. Sacramento, CA: California Youth Authority.

Torres, D.M. 1985. *Gang Violence Reduction Project: Update*. Sacramento, CA: California Youth Authority.

Tremblay, R.E., Masse, L., Pagani, L., and Vitaro, F. 1996. From childhood physical aggression to adolescent maladjustment: The Montreal Prevention Experiment. In *Preventing Childhood Disorders, Substance Abuse, and Delinquency*, edited by R.D. Peters and R.J. McMahon. Thousand Oaks, CA: Sage Publications, Inc.

Trump, K.S. 1996. Gang development and strategies in schools and urban communities. In *Gangs in America*, 2d ed., edited by C.R. Huff. Thousand Oaks, CA: Sage Publications, Inc., pp. 270–280.

Trump, K.S. 1998. *Practical School Security: Basic Guidelines for Safe and Secure Schools*. Thousand Oaks, CA: Corwin Press/Sage Publications, Inc.

U.S. Department of Justice. 1996. Antiviolent crime initiative: The Attorney General's report to the President. Unpublished. Washington, DC: U.S. Department of Justice, Office of the Attorney General.

U.S. General Accounting Office. 1996. *Violent Crime: Federal Law Enforcement Assistance in Fighting Los Angeles Gang Violence*. Washington, DC: U.S. Government Printing Office.

Vila, B., and Meeker, J.W. 1997. A regional gang incident tracking system. *Journal of Gang Research* 4:22–36.

Waldorf, D. 1993. When the Crips invaded San Francisco—gang migration. *Journal of Gang Research* 1:11–16.

Walker, M.L., and Schmidt, L.M. 1996. Gang reduction efforts by the Task Force on Violent Crime in Cleveland, Ohio. In *Gangs in America*, 2d ed., edited by C.R. Huff. Thousand Oaks, CA: Sage Publications, Inc., pp. 263–269.

Watts, R.J. 1991. Manhood development for African-American boys: Program and organization development. Unpublished paper presented at the American Society for Community Research and Action, Tempe, AZ, June.

Weisel, D.L., and Painter, E. 1997. *The Police Response to Gangs: Case Studies of Five Cities*. Washington, DC: Police Executive Research Forum.

Weston, J. 1995. Community policing: An approach to youth gangs in a medium-sized city. In *The Modern Gang Reader*, edited by M.A. Klein, C.L. Maxson, and J. Miller. Los Angeles, CA: Roxbury, pp. 297–300.

Wiebe, D. 1998. Targeting and gang crime: Assessing the impacts of a multi-agency suppression strategy in Orange County, California. Paper presented at the annual meeting of the American Society of Criminology, Washington, DC, November.

Wiebe, D.J., Meeker, J.D., and Vila, B. In press. The Orange County Gang Incident Tracking System: Hourly trends of gang crime incidents, 1995–1998. Washington, DC: U.S. Department of Justice, Office of Justice Programs, National Institute of Justice and the Office of Juvenile Justice and Delinquency Prevention.

Wilson, J.J., and Howell, J.C. 1993. *A Comprehensive Strategy for Serious, Violent, and Chronic Juvenile Offenders.* Washington, DC: U.S. Department of Justice, Office of Justice Programs, Office of Juvenile Justice and Delinquency Prevention.

Winfree, L.T., Esbensen, F., and Osgood, D.W. 1996. Evaluating a school-based gang-prevention program. *Evaluation Review* 20(2):181–203.

Woodson, R.L. 1981. *A Summons to Life: Mediating Structures and the Prevention of Youth Crime.* Cambridge, MA: Ballinger Publishing Company.

Woodson, R.L. 1986. *Gang Mother: The Story of Sister Falaka Fattah.* Elmsford, NY: Pergamon.

Woodson, R.L. 1998. *The Triumphs of Joseph: How Today's Community Healers Are Reviving Our Streets and Neighborhoods.* New York City, NY: The Free Press.

Wyrick, P.A. 2000. *Vietnamese Youth Gang Involvement.* Fact Sheet #200001. Washington, DC: U.S. Department of Justice, Office of Justice Programs, Office of Juvenile Justice and Delinquency Prevention.

Directory of Programs, Strategies, and Organizations

The following is a partial list of programs, strategies, and organizations for which contact information was confirmed at the time of publication. Those marked with an asterisk are no longer in operation.

Aggression Replacement Training (ART)
The Department of Services for Children, Youth and Their Families
1825 Faulkland Road
Wilmington, DE 19805–1195
302–633–2500
thearn@state.de.us

Anti-Gang Office and Task Force, Houston, TX
Mayor's Office
P.O. Box 1562
Houston, TX 77251–1562
713–247–2200

The Beethoven Project
Mike Burke
The Ounce of Prevention Fund
122 South Michigan Avenue, Suite 2050
Chicago, IL 60603
312–922–3863

Big Brothers/Big Sisters of America
Bertha Griffin
Big Brothers/Big Sisters of America National Headquarters
230 North 13th Street
Philadelphia, PA 19107
215–567–7000

Bloomington/Normal Comprehensive Community-Wide Approach to Gang Prevention, Intervention, and Suppression*
Patrick Morland, Executive Director
702 South Morris
Bloomington, IL 60701
309–827–8282

Blythe Street Gang Injunction*
American Civil Liberties Union of Southern California
1616 Beverly Boulevard
Los Angeles, CA 90026
213–977–9500

Boston Gun Project
Dorchester District Court
510 Washington Street
Dorchester, MA 02124
617–288–9500

Boys & Girls Clubs of America
National Headquarters
1230 West Peachtree Street NW.
Atlanta, GA 30309
404–815–5700
lmclemore@bgca.org

Broader Urban Involvement and Leadership Development (BUILD)
David Yancy
1223 North Milwaukee Avenue
Chicago, IL 60622
312–227–2880
build@surfnetcorp.net

Cease Fire
Sergeant Robert Heimberger
St. Louis Metropolitan Police Department
1200 Clark Boulevard
St. Louis, MO 63103
314–444–5681

Chicago Area Project (CAP)
David Whitaker
200 South Michigan Avenue, Suite 1400
Chicago, IL 60604
312–663–3574

Child Development-Community Policing (CD–CP)
Colleen Valdala, Administrative Assistant
Yale Child Study Center
47 College Street, Suite 212
New Haven, CT 06510
203–785–7047

Comin' Up
Angela Ware, Director
Crime Prevention Resource Center
Boys & Girls Club
605 East Berry Street
Fort Worth, TX 76110
817–923–5472

Collaborative Intensive Community Treatment Program
Perseus House
1946 West 26th Street
Erie, PA 16508
814–453–7909
perseus@erie.net

Communities In Schools (CIS)
277 South Washington Street, Suite 210
Alexandria, VA 22314–1436
703–519–8999
cis@cisnet.org

Community Action Team (CAT)
Reno (NV) Police Department
455 East Second Street
Reno, NV 89101
775–334–2108

The Community Outreach Program
St. Paul (MN) Police Department
100 East 11th Street
St. Paul, MN 55101
651–291–1111

Community Resources Against Street Hoodlums (CRASH)*
Career Criminal Apprehension Section
Los Angeles (CA) Police Department
150 North Los Angeles Street
Los Angeles, CA 90012
213–437–8103

Comprehensive Strategy for Serious, Violent, and Chronic Juvenile Offenders
Mark Matese
Office of Juvenile Justice and
    Delinquency Prevention
810 Seventh Street NW., Third Floor
Washington, DC 20531
202–616–9870

Consent to Search and Seize
Sergeant Robert Heimberger
St. Louis Metropolitan Police Department
1200 Clark Boulevard
St. Louis, MO 63103
314–444–5681

Early Intervention Program
Orange County Probation Department
909 North Main Street
Santa Ana, CA 92701–3511
714–569–2000

El Puente ("The Bridge")
Ingrid Mateas
211 South 4th Street
Brooklyn, NY 11211
718–387–0404

Empowerment Zones
Community Connections
P.O. Box 7189
Gaithersburg, MD 20898–7189
800–998–9999
800–483–2209 (TDD)
301–519–5027 (fax)
comcon@aspsensys.com

Enterprise Communities
Community Connections
P.O. Box 7189
Gaithersburg, MD 20898–7189
800–998–9999
800–483–2209 (TDD)
301–519–5027 (fax)
comcon@aspsensys.com

Firearm Suppression Program (FSP)
Sergeant Robert Heimberger
St. Louis Metropolitan Police Department
1200 Clark Boulevard
St. Louis, MO 63103
314–444–5681

Gang Awareness Necessary for Growth in Society (GANGS)
California Youth Authority
4241 Williamsbourgh Drive
Sacramento, CA 95823
916–262–1480

Gang Incident Tracking System (GITS)
James Meeker
Criminology, Law and Society
University of California, Irvine
Irvine, CA 92697
949–824–7306

Gang Peace/First
Rodney Dailey
Gang Peace, Inc.
318 Blue Hill Avenue
Roxbury, MA 02121
617–989–1285

Gang Prevention and Intervention Program
Youth Development, Inc.
6301 Central NW.
Albuquerque, NM 87105
505–831–6038

Gang Prevention Through Targeted Outreach, Boys & Girls Clubs of America
Frank Sanchez, Jr.
Senior Director of Delinquency Prevention
Boys & Girls Clubs of America
1230 West Peachtree Street NW.
Atlanta, GA 30309
404–487–5907

Gang Rehabilitation, Assessment, and Services Program (GRAASP)*
San Antonio Police Department
214 West Nueva Street
San Antonio, TX 78207
210–207–7615

Gang Resistance Education and Training Program (G.R.E.A.T.)
Bureau of Alcohol, Tobacco and Firearms
650 Massachusetts Avenue NW.
Washington, DC 20226
800–726–7070
202–927–2160

Gang Resistance Is Paramount (G.R.I.P.)
Tony Ostos
Neighborhood Counseling Manager, G.R.I.P.
16400 Colorado Avenue
Paramount, CA 90723–5050
562–220–2120

Gang Victim Services Program
Lamoreaux Justice Center
341 The City Drive
Orange, CA 92866
714–935–7492

Golden Eagles
Julie Green
Minneapolis American Indian Center
1530 East Franklin Avenue
Minneapolis, MN 55404
612–879–1708

Gulf Coast Trades Center
Oscar Gonzales, Admissions Administrator
Gulf Coast Trades Center
P.O. Box 515
New Waverly, TX 77358
409–344–6677

High/Scope Perry Preschool Project
Lawrence Schweinhart, Ph.D.
600 North River Street
Ypsilanti, MI 48198
734–485–2000

Homeboy Industries
Greg Boyle
1848 East First Street
Los Angeles, CA 90033
323–526–1254

House of Umoja
Sister Falaka Fattah
1410 North Frazer Street
Philadelphia, PA 19131
215–473–5893

Information Collection for Automated Mapping (ICAM)
Chicago Police Department Research and
  Development Division
3510 South Michigan
Chicago, IL 60653
312–747–6204

Inner-City Games (ICG)
Harley Frankel
National Office
1460 4th Street, Suite 300
Santa Monica, CA 90401
310–458–4411

Jobs for a Future
Greg Boyle
1848 East First Street
Los Angeles, CA 90033
323–526–1254

Jurisdictions Unified for Drug Gang Enforcement (JUDGE)
Robert Amador, Deputy District Attorney
2901 Meadow Lark Drive
San Diego, CA 92123
858–694–4790

Lifeskills '95
P.O. Box 9490
San Bernardino, CA 92427
909–880–2577

Little Village Gang Violence Reduction Program⁎
Tracy Hahn
Illinois Criminal Justice Information Authority
120 South Riverside Plaza, Suite 1016
Chicago, IL 60606–3997
312–793–8647
thahn@icjia.state.il.us

Mesa Gang Intervention Project (MGIP)
Kimo Souza
540 West Broadway Road, Suite 108
Mesa, AZ 85210
480–644–4370

Minnesota HEALS (Hope, Education, and Law and Safety)
Pat Hoven
1621 West 25th Street
Minneapolis, MN 55405
612–374–2589
phovey@earthlink.net

Mobile Enforcement Team (MET)
Drug Enforcement Administration
Information Services Section
700 Army Navy Drive
Arlington, VA 22202
202–307–7977

Neighborhood Watch
P.O. Box 4208
Santa Fe Springs, CA 90670
888–669–4872

The Neutral Zone
5409 228th Street SW.
Mountlake Terrace, WA 98043
425–670–2875

Norfolk Police Assisted Community Enforcement
PACE
Marty Raiss
501 Boush Street
Norfolk, VA 23510
757–441–2400

Nuestro Centro*
Texas Youth Commission
4900 North Lamar Boulevard
Austin, TX 78751
Post Office Box 4260
Austin, TX 78765
512–424–6130

Operation Ceasefire
Jim Jordan, Director
Office of Strategic Planning and
   Resource Development
Boston Police Department
1 Schroeder Plaza
Boston, MA 02120
617–343–4507

Operation Hardcore
Hardcore Gang Division
210 West Temple Street, Room 17–1116
Los Angeles, CA 90012
213–974–3903

Operation Night Light
Boston Program
Dorchester District Court
510 Washington Street
Dorchester, MA 02124
617–288–9500

St. Louis Program
Sergeant Robert Heimberger
St. Louis Metropolitan Police Department
1200 Clark Boulevard
St. Louis, MO 63103
314–444–5681

Operation Safe Streets
3010 East Victoria Street
Rancho Dominguez, CA 90221
310–603–3100

**Parents and Schools Succeeding in Providing
Organized Routes to Travel (PASSPORT)***
Ralph Lomeli, Safe Schools Coordinator
Visalia Unified School District
315 East Acequia
Visalia, CA 93291
559–730–7579

Partnership for a Safer Cleveland
Michael Walker
614 Superior Avenue West, Suite 1110
Cleveland, OH 44113
216–523–1128
216–523–1823 (fax)
walkerohio@aol.com

Project RAISE
Richard Rowe
Baltimore Mentoring Partnership
605 Eutaw Street
Baltimore, MD 21201
410–685–8316
410–752–5016 (fax)

Project Save-A-Youth
Deborah Moore
Community Services Department
200 South Anaheim Boulevard, Suite 433
Anaheim, CA 92805
714–254–5246

**Riverside's Comprehensive Community-Wide
Approach to Gang Prevention, Intervention,
and Suppression**
Riverside (CA) Police Department
4102 Orange Street
Riverside, CA 92501
909–782–5550

Strategies Against Gang Environments (SAGE)*
LA County District Attorney's Office
Bureau of Crime Prevention
210 West Temple Street, Room 18000
Los Angeles, CA 90012
213–974–3512

Teens on Target (TNT)
3300 Elm Street
Oakland, CA 94609
510–594–2588
510–594–0667 (fax)

Tri-Agency Resource Gang Enforcement Team (TARGET)
Bill Smith
City of Westminster
8200 Westminster Boulevard
Westminster, CA 92683
714–898–3311

Tucson Gang Project*
John Basquez Bedoy
Karen Pugh
OUR Town Family Center
P.O. Box 26665
Tucson, AZ 85726
520–323–1708
520–323–9077 (fax)

Violence-Free Zones
Main and Administrative Office
2908 Madeline Street
Oakland, CA 94602
510–530–1319
510–530–1527 (fax)

Branch Office
P.O. Box 181
Moraga, CA 94556
925–376–3237
925–376–2386 (fax)

Youth Firearms Violence Initiative, Inglewood, CA*
Lieutenant Hampton Cantrell
Inglewood Police Department
1 Manchester Boulevard
Inglewood, CA 90301
310–412–5206
310–412–8798 (fax)

Youth Firearms Violence Initiative, Milwaukee, WI*
Lieutenant James Galezewski
Milwaukee Police Department
749 West State Street
Milwaukee, WI 53233
414–935–7825

Youth Firearms Violence Initiative, Salinas, CA
Sergeant Tracy Molfino
Salinas Police Department
222 Lincoln Avenue
Salinas, CA 93901–2639
831–758–7348

Youth Firearms Violence Initiative, Seattle, WA*
Julie Baker, Grant Coordinator
Community Information and
  Services Bureau
Seattle Police Department
610 Third Avenue
Seattle, WA 98104
206–233–5133

Youth Violence Strike Force, Baltimore, MD
Sergeant William Marcus
Baltimore City Police Department
Violent Crimes Division
601 East Fayette Street, Mezzanine
Baltimore, MD 21202
410–396–2650

Index of Programs, Strategies, and Organizations*

*This index does not include some of the programs in table 1, pages 3–4.

Publications From OJJDP

OJJDP produces a variety of publications—Fact Sheets, Bulletins, Summaries, Reports, and the *Juvenile Justice* journal—along with videotapes, including broadcasts from the juvenile justice telecommunications initiative. Through OJJDP's Juvenile Justice Clearinghouse (JJC), these publications and other resources are as close as your phone, fax, computer, or mailbox.

Phone:

800–638–8736
(Monday–Friday, 8:30 a.m.–7 p.m. ET)

Fax:

410–792–4358 (to order publications)
301–519–5600 (to ask questions)

Online:

OJJDP Home Page:

www.ojjdp.ncjrs.org

To Order Materials:

www.ncjrs.org/puborder

E-Mail:

askncjrs@ncjrs.org (to ask questions about materials)

Mail:

Juvenile Justice Clearinghouse/NCJRS
P.O. Box 6000, Rockville, MD 20849–6000

Fact Sheets and Bulletins are also available through fax-on-demand.

Fax-on-Demand:

800–638–8736, select option 1, select option 2, and listen for instructions.

To ensure timely notice of new publications, subscribe to JUVJUST, OJJDP's electronic mailing list.

JUVJUST Mailing List:

E-mail to listproc@ncjrs.org
Leave the subject line blank
Type *subscribe juvjust your name*

In addition, JJC, through the National Criminal Justice Reference Service (NCJRS), is the repository for tens of thousands of criminal and juvenile justice publications and resources from around the world. They are abstracted and placed in a database, which is searchable online (www.ncjrs.org/database.htm). You are also welcome to submit materials to JJC for inclusion in the database.

The following list highlights popular and recently published OJJDP documents and videotapes, grouped by topical areas.

The OJJDP Publications List (BC000115) offers a complete list of OJJDP publications and is also available online.

In addition, the OJJDP Fact Sheet Flier (LT000333) offers a complete list of OJJDP Fact Sheets and is available online.

OJJDP also sponsors a teleconference initiative, and a flier (LT116) offers a complete list of videos available from these broadcasts.

Corrections and Detention

Beyond the Walls: Improving Conditions of Confinement for Youth in Custody. 1998, NCJ 164727 (116 pp.).

Disproportionate Minority Confinement: 1997 Update. 1998, NCJ 170606 (12 pp.).

Disproportionate Minority Confinement: Lessons Learned From Five States. 1998, NCJ 173420 (12 pp.).

Juvenile Arrests 1997. 1999, NCJ 173938 (12 pp.).

Reintegration, Supervised Release, and Intensive Aftercare. 1999, NCJ 175715 (24 pp.).

Courts

Guide for Implementing the Balanced and Restorative Justice Model. 1998. NCJ 167887 (112 pp.).

Innovative Approaches to Juvenile Indigent Defense. 1998, NCJ 171151 (8 pp.).

Juvenile Court Statistics 1996. 1999, NCJ 168963 (113 pp.).

Offenders in Juvenile Court, 1996. 1999, NCJ 175719 (12 pp.).

RESTTA National Directory of Restitution and Community Service Programs. 1998, NCJ 166365 (500 pp.), $33.50.

Trying Juveniles as Adults in Criminal Court: An Analysis of State Transfer Provisions. 1998, NCJ 172836 (112 pp.).

Youth Courts: A National Movement Teleconference (Video). 1998, NCJ 171149 (120 min.), $17.

Delinquency Prevention

1998 Report to Congress: Juvenile Mentoring Program (JUMP). 1999, NCJ 173424 (65 pp.).

1998 Report to Congress: Title V Incentive Grants for Local Delinquency Prevention Programs. 1999, NCJ 176342 (58 pp.).

Combating Violence and Delinquency: The National Juvenile Justice Action Plan (Report). 1996, NCJ 157106 (200 pp.).

Combating Violence and Delinquency: The National Juvenile Justice Action Plan (Summary). 1996, NCJ 157105 (36 pp.).

Effective Family Strengthening Interventions. 1998, NCJ 171121 (16 pp.).

Juvenile Accountability Incentive Block Grants Strategic Planning Guide. 1999, NCJ 172846 (62 pp.).

Parents Anonymous: Strengthening America's Families. 1999, NCJ 171120 (12 pp.).

Prenatal and Early Childhood Nurse Home Visitation. 1998, NCJ 172875 (8 pp.).

Treatment Foster Care. 1999, NCJ 173421 (12 pp.).

Gangs

1996 National Youth Gang Survey. 1999, NCJ 173964 (96 pp.).

Gang Members on the Move. 1998, NCJ 171153 (12 pp.).

Youth Gangs: An Overview. 1998, NCJ 167249 (20 pp.).

The Youth Gangs, Drugs, and Violence Connection. 1999, NCJ 171152 (12 pp.).

Youth Gangs in America Teleconference (Video). 1997, NCJ 164937 (120 min.), $17.

General Juvenile Justice

Comprehensive Juvenile Justice in State Legislatures Teleconference (Video). 1998, NCJ 169593 (120 min.), $17.

Guidelines for the Screening of Persons Working With Children, the Elderly, and Individuals With Disabilities in Need of Support. 1998, NCJ 167248 (52 pp.).

Juvenile Justice, Volume VII, Number 1. 2000, NCJ 178256 (40 pp.).

A Juvenile Justice System for the 21st Century. 1998, NCJ 169726 (8 pp.).

Juvenile Offenders and Victims: 1999 National Report. 1999, NCJ 178257 (232 pp.).

OJJDP Research: Making a Difference for Juveniles. 1999, NCJ 177602 (52 pp.).

Promising Strategies To Reduce Gun Violence. 1999, NCJ 173950 (253 pp.).

Sharing Information: A Guide to the Family Educational Rights and Privacy Act and Participation in Juvenile Justice Programs. 1997, NCJ 163705 (52 pp.).

Missing and Exploited Children

Portable Guides to Investigating Child Abuse (13-title series).

Protecting Children Online Teleconference (Video). 1998, NCJ 170023 (120 min.), $17.

When Your Child Is Missing: A Family Survival Guide. 1998, NCJ 170022 (96 pp.).

Substance Abuse

The Coach's Playbook Against Drugs. 1998, NCJ 173393 (20 pp.).

Drug Identification and Testing in the Juvenile Justice System. 1998, NCJ 167889 (92 pp.).

Preparing for the Drug Free Years. 1999, NCJ 173408 (12 pp.).

Violence and Victimization

Combating Fear and Restoring Safety in Schools. 1998, NCJ 167888 (16 pp.).

Guide for Implementing the Comprehensive Strategy for Serious, Violent, and Chronic Juvenile Offenders. 1995, NCJ 153681 (255 pp.).

Report to Congress on Juvenile Violence Research. 1999, NCJ 176976 (44 pp.).

Serious and Violent Juvenile Offenders. 1998, NCJ 170027 (8 pp.).

Serious and Violent Juvenile Offenders: Risk Factors and Successful Interventions Teleconference (Video). 1998, NCJ 171286 (120 min.), $17.

State Legislative Responses to Violent Juvenile Crime: 1996–97 Update. 1998, NCJ 172835 (16 pp.).

White House Conference on School Safety: Causes and Prevention of Youth Violence Teleconference (Video). 1998, NCJ 173399 (240 min.), $17.

Youth in Action

Community Cleanup. 1999, NCJ 171690 (6 pp.).

Cross-Age Teaching. 1999, NCJ 171688 (8 pp.).

Make a Friend—Be a Peer Mentor. 1999, NCJ 171691 (8 pp.).

Plan A Special Event! 1999, NCJ 171689 (8 pp.).

Planning a Successful Crime Prevention Project. 1998, NCJ 170024 (28 pp.).

Stand Up and Start a School Crime Watch! 1998, NCJ 171123 (8 pp.)

Two Generations—Partners in Prevention. 1999, NCJ 171687 (8 pp.).

Wipe Out Vandalism and Graffiti. 1998, NCJ 171122 (8 pp.).

Youth Preventing Drug Abuse. 1998, NCJ 171124 (8 pp.).

www.ingramcontent.com/pod-product-compliance
Lightning Source LLC
Chambersburg PA
CBHW081228280526
45787CB00006B/2575